Bible Word Search Puzzles

TEST YOUR BIBLE KNOWLEDGE

Publications International, Ltd.

Jeanette Dall is a freelance writer and former elementary school teacher who has written stories, puzzles, and games for children and adults. She has contributed to many educational and religious publications, including *Bible Adventures*, *Circle Time Activities*, and *Apples for the Teacher*.

Cliff Leitch is an engineer by trade, but a Bible scholar at heart. He maintains TwoPaths.com, a Christian Bible study Web site, for which he writes and compiles Bible facts, puzzles, and games.

Randy Petersen is a freelance writer and editor who has contributed to more than 20 religious titles, including *The Revell Bible Dictionary* and *The Life & Times of Jesus*. In addition, he has contributed to books such as *Best Loved Bible Verses*, *The Christian Book of Lists*, and *The Family Book of Bible Fun*.

Louis Weber, CEO
Publications International, Ltd.
7373 North Cicero Avenue
Lincolnwood, Illinois 60712

Permission is never granted for commercial purposes.

ISBN-13: 978-0-7853-9317-7
ISBN-10: 0-7853-9317-X

Manufactured in USA

8 7 6 5 4 3 2 1

WELCOME

There are many reasons why the Bible is the best-selling book of all time. For believers it has been a source of wisdom and inspiration for thousands of years. It contains a fascinating wealth of details about the people, places, and events of biblical times. Today, the Bible continues to be a dynamic book that can be read again and again, each time bringing new insight and understanding.

Bible Word Search Puzzles is an interesting tool to test your biblical knowledge—and help you learn more in the process. This book points you to fascinating facts and phenomena from the NRSV Bible (it's actually a good idea to keep a copy nearby as you work on the puzzles). In all the word searches, you'll look for words diagonally, vertically, horizontally, backward, and forward. And while you are welcome to open the book to any page, you should know that word searches near the beginning of the book tend to be easier than the ones near the end. In fact, we've made some of the last puzzles more difficult by asking you to also solve fill-in-the-blanks, quiz questions, unscrambles, and more. Thankfully, no matter your skill level, you will find all the answers on the last few pages.

You'll have a great time whether you're going through this book alone, with a friend, or in a group. Good luck, and have fun!

On the Job 〰〰〰〰〰〰〰〰〰〰〰〰〰〰〰〰〰

Fifteen biblical occupations are hidden in this grid. Can you do the job of finding them? Answers on page 67.

Carpenter	Judge	Silversmith
Farmer	Magi	Tax Collector
Fisher	Merchant	Teacher
Hunter	Priest	Tentmaker
Innkeeper	Shepherd	Warrior

```
M  S  S  I  L  V  E  R  S  M  I  T  H  U  H
C  N  W  D  Q  V  J  U  D  G  E  C  C  G  B
V  D  Q  D  J  R  L  I  V  U  S  V  I  P  W
C  R  H  B  R  H  Y  A  H  U  D  G  P  A  A
C  O  Z  J  I  E  O  O  W  J  A  K  Q  A  R
Z  T  G  J  T  I  H  H  N  M  B  Q  H  J  R
T  C  L  R  C  E  U  P  G  P  R  V  K  M  I
E  E  P  P  E  N  N  P  E  F  N  D  O  E  O
A  L  C  Y  T  H  E  T  A  H  O  Z  D  R  R
C  L  Q  E  S  H  S  R  M  B  S  J  D  C  T
H  O  R  J  R  X  M  I  J  A  I  Q  J  H  S
E  C  B  K  G  E  N  V  F  P  K  G  Y  A  E
R  X  O  R  R  O  T  M  D  T  U  E  O  N  I
N  A  R  E  T  N  E  P  R  A  C  B  R  T  R
I  T  I  N  N  K  E  E  P  E  R  R  I  K  P
```

Water, water everywhere. Much of the Bible occurred in an arid climate; maybe that's why the rivers and seas were so important. Try to find 15 biblical bodies of water in this word search. Answers on page 67.

```
A  G  F  E  U  P  H  R  A  T  E  S  A  N  M  U
E  D  O  N  O  N  O  R  D  I  K  D  O  H  C  L
S  N  A  N  U  A  M  Y  Y  H  I  B  G  L  E  G
D  A  G  R  N  E  E  N  J  A  A  A  A  N  S  L
A  E  A  X  O  A  D  S  S  K  L  M  L  Q  M  O
E  N  K  C  R  J  D  H  D  I  N  S  F  A  C  B
D  A  A  N  X  I  T  R  L  E  L  D  O  N  V  S
A  R  Z  J  L  E  C  E  O  A  R  L  I  K  Z  I
E  R  Y  U  B  W  E  B  G  J  I  I  O  S  D  R
L  E  F  K  B  K  A  F  U  S  O  B  C  B  U  G
I  T  D  H  Z  L  M  V  X  W  B  A  L  W  I  I
N  I  U  Z  G  R  Q  V  A  A  J  T  F  A  B  T
B  D  P  H  E  L  Q  X  J  H  I  J  S  B  X  T
O  E  U  S  D  F  B  C  F  H  A  H  C  E  T  W
U  M  G  F  U  L  N  O  H  I  G  B  U  J  X  H
L  S  K  R  B  V  H  T  I  R  E  H  C  K  A  F
```

Ahava	Euphrates	Jordan	Red Sea
Bethsaida	Galilee	Kidron	Siloam
Cherith	Gihon	Mediterranean	Tigris
Dead Sea	Jabbok	Nile	

There's Music in the Air

Biblical people were a musical group. Search for the 14 entries here. Answers on page 67.

```
P R A I H O R N S S L Y R E T U L F E
S T R I N G E D I N S T R U M E N T S
H T O S E N I R U O B M A T P T H H B
E A L O R O D U C Y M B A L S I G A E
O D R A L G M M T R U M P E T S P I L
G H T P G N O S T E N A T S A C Y E L
```

Bell	Flute	Lyre	Stringed Instruments
Castanets	Gong	Pipe	
Cymbals	Harp	Song	Tambourines
Drums	Horns		Trumpets

It's Empty

Look for the 16 Easter-related words. Answers on page 67.

Alive	Jesus	Mary	Salome
Angel	Joy	Peter	Stone
Dawn	Love	Ran	Tomb
Fear	Magdalene	Risen	Women

```
J L O V E J I P E T E R
A N G E L G E Q F A F W
N E D R Y M D B E J E O
A N N O O A A M V J A M
R O J L S R W O I E R E
W T A K H Y N T L S L N
T S N E S I R W A U O P
E N E L A D G A M S V O
```

The Bible speaks about spiritual gifts: abilities that believers have in order to strengthen one another and glorify God. There are a few lists of these gifts, mainly in Romans 12, 1 Corinthians 12, and Ephesians 4. Find the 16 gifts in this puzzle. Answers on page 67.

```
H  N  T  E  A  C  H  I  N  G  P  A  U  O  H  R
R  O  H  T  N  E  M  N  R  E  C  S  I  D  B  S
O  T  I  E  F  U  Y  C  E  H  P  O  R  P  S  I
H  T  C  G  X  V  S  M  G  W  T  P  I  E  L  N
F  Y  L  L  A  H  E  E  G  I  L  Z  N  I  E  T
G  R  E  E  E  R  O  N  U  Q  V  L  H  M  A  E
N  T  Y  G  R  D  I  R  W  G  U  I  I  C  D  R
I  S  Y  T  D  W  D  I  T  F  N  R  N  F  E  P
L  I  Y  I  R  E  S  G  R  A  A  O  K  G  R  R
A  N  G  E  F  D  L  E  M  C  T  H  T  G  S  E
E  I  T  Q  O  I  E  W  L  R  N  I  Q  F  H  T
H  M  O  M  H  H  G  E  O  P  C  D  O  V  I  A
X  F  C  N  C  P  S  F  T  N  D  G  V  N  P  T
I  A  F  C  K  K  W  K  V  J  K  G  Q  C  W  I
J  P  O  F  A  I  T  H  V  O  B  H  O  A  H  O
A  B  O  E  V  A  N  G  E  L  I  S  M  O  S  N
```

Cheerfulness	Faith	Knowledge	Prophecy
Discernment	Giving	Leadership	Teaching
Evangelism	Healing	Ministry	Tongues
Exhortation	Interpretation	Miracles	Wisdom

Tree's Company

Sometimes, when studying Scripture, you can't see the forest for the trees. The following forest of a puzzle has a variety of trees and a few flowers too—19 in all. Answers on page 67.

Almond	Fir	Oak	Rose
Cedar	Henna	Olive	Saffron
Cypress	Lily	Palm	Sycamore
Ebony	Myrtle	Pine	Willow
Fig	Nard	Poplar	

```
P  P  O  P  L  A  R  X  V  F  F  I  R  B  F  O
L  J  U  U  S  O  O  L  F  A  V  I  W  F  R  O
I  R  I  N  W  U  A  R  W  E  D  F  Q  O  N  L
N  E  D  V  J  J  F  O  A  S  S  U  F  K  P  I
E  B  W  A  G  E  L  G  R  O  S  L  W  I  E  V
R  O  O  L  V  L  N  A  L  R  E  Q  J  S  L  E
D  N  B  A  I  D  D  I  F  U  R  M  E  C  T  C
N  Y  T  W  S  E  Y  N  P  W  P  R  T  H  R  L
O  D  I  T  C  C  V  F  C  R  Y  S  A  N  Y  I
M  F  Y  J  W  D  P  D  H  M  C  C  F  P  M  L
L  I  G  K  F  B  Y  C  L  E  N  U  W  E  B  Y
A  G  O  P  K  X  D  A  A  X  N  G  L  O  S  D
O  I  M  A  J  T  P  O  X  D  H  N  P  B  F  R
Y  H  H  X  K  C  M  V  B  M  E  N  A  V  X  A
W  S  P  P  B  E  R  O  M  A  C  Y  S  S  E  N
K  D  C  G  P  N  O  R  F  F  A  S  M  R  D  P
```

The Bible is an absolute zoo. Of course God created all the animals in Genesis, but then they keep popping up later. We've put 20 of them in this word search. (Don't know what a behemoth or a leviathan is? Look them up in Job 40:15 and Job 41:1.) Answers on page 67.

```
R  O  G  Z  H  Y  N  P  X  E  L  X  O  C  B
U  E  R  E  E  D  Y  N  E  M  P  F  L  O  V
F  G  P  I  Y  L  R  E  Y  E  L  A  J  D  N
G  O  R  Q  C  U  E  P  K  O  H  D  S  N  V
O  D  Y  S  S  X  V  M  W  N  R  S  D  C  R
A  O  E  R  H  B  W  I  A  A  O  S  Y  A  E
T  W  S  O  X  F  Y  P  P  C  B  D  A  T  L
H  H  R  U  X  V  U  O  I  E  F  R  E  T  T
T  A  O  F  V  E  E  J  H  G  P  B  M  L  A
E  R  H  O  T  L  N  E  X  H  F  X  E  E  B
A  E  G  H  N  H  M  K  C  N  I  O  F  A  L
A  X  D  N  O  O  P  Y  R  S  Q  O  A  P  R
M  W  S  P  T  F  L  E  V  I  A  T  H  A  N
L  G  Z  H  W  T  O  K  S  M  L  I  O  N  Q
V  J  A  X  P  V  K  X  L  C  C  T  M  F  M
```

Ape	Cattle	Goat	Lion
Bat	Deer	Hare	Oxen
Bear	Dog	Horse	Pig
Behemoth	Donkey	Leopard	Sheep
Camel	Fox	Leviathan	Wolf

The Traveling Man

The first missionary, Paul, traveled all over the Mediterranean world spreading the Good News. Find the 21 names of some of the cities he visited. Answers on page 68.

Antioch	Derbe	Lystra	Tarsus
Apollonia	Ephesus	Perga	Thessalonica
Athens	Fair Havens	Philippi	Troas
Caesarea	Iconium	Rome	
Colossae	Issus	Smyrna	
Damascus	Jerusalem	Syracuse	

```
S  P  E  R  G  A  R  T  S  Y  L  R  A
A  N  T  I  O  C  H  G  A  S  N  C  S
E  R  W  Y  E  A  S  O  L  L  O  C  M
T  D  A  M  A  S  C  U  S  U  A  S  Y
H  R  I  C  O  N  I  U  M  E  T  U  R
E  J  O  A  T  H  E  N  S  A  M  S  N
S  I  M  A  L  Z  O  A  G  E  V  E  A
S  S  X  I  S  L  R  T  L  D  P  H  I
A  I  H  P  L  E  L  A  P  I  H  P  P
L  S  B  M  A  N  S  L  B  O  D  E  P
O  S  Z  K  O  U  E  M  O  R  F  B  I
N  U  S  Y  R  A  C  U  S  E  S  R  L
I  S  N  E  V  A  H  R  I  A  F  E  I
C  A  J  H  T  A  R  S  U  S  C  D  H
A  P  O  L  L  O  N  I  A  D  A  H  P
```

Jesus was called many names; 21 of those names are in this puzzle. Answers on page 68.

```
G  O  O  D  S  H  E  P  H  E  R  D  N  J  E
D  L  R  O  W  E  H  T  F  O  T  H  G  I  L
B  P  Y  G  L  O  R  D  S  C  H  R  I  S  T
L  N  I  L  R  L  N  O  O  A  T  G  I  L  D
I  G  A  K  E  S  O  G  N  G  E  E  T  A  M
L  N  H  H  B  E  I  F  O  M  A  F  E  I  L
E  O  A  I  C  R  T  O  F  W  C  M  A  W  Q
U  H  I  M  R  V  C  N  M  K  H  E  A  P  A
N  K  S  E  R  A  E  O  A  I  E  Y  N  T  H
A  J  S  O  D  N  R  S  N  B  R  A  Y  F  A
M  K  E  O  V  T  R  S  T  R  U  T  H  A  G
M  T  M  S  I  N  U  S  E  W  A  T  A  D  T
E  W  Y  U  U  R  S  E  N  M  O  L  I  F  S
A  T  V  P  T  S  E  J  I  V  I  N  S  Z  E
H  E  M  H  P  O  R  D  V  E  L  P  S  P  M
L  I  V  I  N  G  W  A  T  E  R  L  O  J  O
D  P  F  C  O  X  A  O  H  M  L  K  I  N  G
L  T  Z  M  S  N  W  T  E  M  P  L  E  F  M
E  F  I  L  F  O  D  A  E  R  B  A  S  A  E
```

Bread of Life	King	Messiah	Teacher
Christ	Life	Resurrection	Temple
Emmanuel	Light of the World	Servant	Truth
Good Shepherd		Son	Vine
	Living Water	Son of God	Way
Jesus	Lord	Son of Man	

Tremendous T's

Search for these 22 words that begin with the letter T. Answers on page 68.

```
T  D  E  R  U  G  I  F  S  N  A  R  T  R  U  T  H
R  A  D  I  T  L  N  F  E  H  T  I  T  O  E  P  O
E  T  A  B  E  R  N  A  C  L  E  I  K  Q  W  G  J
E  L  P  M  E  T  U  C  H  M  M  T  A  B  L  E  T
B  T  O  N  G  U  E  S  P  O  P  S  E  X  A  T  R
S  K  N  A  H  T  S  U  T  H  T  T  I  T  U  S  B
                  W  W  H  R  C  A  C
                  E  Y  V  A  A  T  E
                  L  O  Z  N  E  I  A
                  V  S  X  S  T  O  L
                  E  E  T  G  A  N  L
                  L  S  H  R  L  Y  E
                  W  S  O  E  E  M  T
                  R  A  M  S  N  D  L
                  E  P  A  S  T  G  X
                  N  S  S  I  S  S  M
                  G  E  E  O  I  K  O
                  U  R  V  N  T  N  H
                  S  T  L  E  I  A  E
```

Tabernacle			Transfigured
Tablet			Transgression
Talents			Tree
Taxes	Temptation	Tithe	Trespasses
Teach	Thanks	Titus	Trust
Tell	Thomas	Tongues	Truth
Temple	Timothy	Tower	Twelve

Powerful *P*'s

There are lots of **P** *words in the Old and New Testaments. Twenty-three of them are in this word search. Answers on page 68.*

```
P  A  P  A  R  A  B  L  E  R  P  B  C
R  T  E  H  P  O  R  P  E  E  H  P  D
O  P  R  P  A  L  M  T  E  F  I  H  E
V  R  S  P  G  H  E  I  I  L  L  A  T
E  I  E  E  K  P  T  J  P  U  I  R  S
R  E  V  O  S  S  A  P  A  A  P  I  O
B  S  E  P  E  A  L  R  R  P  P  S  C
E  T  R  L  S  L  I  A  E  U  I  E  E
U  S  A  E  I  M  P  Y  N  R  A  E  T
G  N  N  L  A  S  M  E  T  E  N  S  N
A  S  C  R  R  Q  P  R  S  O  S  N  E
L  T  E  U  P  E  C  N  E  I  T  A  P
P  H  A  R  A  O  H  V  E  C  A  E  P
```

Palm	People	Praise
Parable	Perseverance	Prayer
Parents	Peter	Priests
Passover	Pharaoh	Prophet
Patience	Pharisees	Proverb
Paul	Philippians	Psalms
Peace	Pilate	Pure
Pentecost	Plague	

Follow Me ∽∽∽∽∽∽∽∽∽∽∽∽∽∽∽∽∽∽∽∽∽∽∽∽∽

> *Many people followed Jesus as he traveled and taught. Find these 23 followers. Answers on page 68.*

Andrew

Blind Beggar

Cleopas

James

Joanna

John

Joseph of Arimathea

Jude

Lazarus

Leper

Luke

Martha

Mary

Mary Magdalene

Matthew

Nathanael

Nicodemus

Peter

Philip

Salome

Simon of Cyrene

Thomas

Zacchaeus

```
          T  A  R  N  O  M  N  S
          B  S  N  E  H  A  B  E
          N  I  X  D  T  O  O  M
          D  M  L  H  R  E  J  A
          E  O  A  J  Y  E  P  J
    P  E  K  U  L  R  N  C  O  R  N  W  J  O  A  N  N  A
    M  A  R  T  H  A  O  L  S  A  E  Z  T  M  L  S  X  Q
    L  J  U  D  E  T  F  L  E  M  L  A  Z  A  R  U  S  O
    P  H  I  L  I  P  C  E  P  N  A  C  L  E  O  P  A  S
    H  L  C  E  B  P  Y  P  H  I  D  C  E  M  O  L  A  S
          R  R  E  O  C  G  H  N
          A  E  R  F  O  A  A  T
          G  N  A  A  D  M  E  Z
          G  E  G  R  E  Y  U  A
          E  W  G  I  M  R  S  C
          B  E  J  M  U  A  A  L
          D  H  B  A  S  M  M  O
          N  T  D  T  I  S  O  J
          I  T  N  H  L  M  H  A
          L  A  D  E  C  M  T  A
          B  M  L  A  M  A  R  R
```

Tired of the Tabernacle, King David wanted to build God a house, a more permanent temple where the people could worship. It was his son Solomon who made it happen. Find these 24 pertinent story details (from 1 Kings 6–7) below. Answers on page 68.

Altar	Cypress	Oxen	Shovels
Ark of the Covenant	Doorposts	Palm Trees	Solomon
	Gold	Pillars	Stands
Beams	Hiram	Pomegranates	Stone
Carvings	Olivewood	Pots	Wheels
Cedar	Overlaid	Sea	Wings
Cherub			

```
S  A  N  S  R  A  L  L  I  P  R  U  B  B  H  Y
L  R  B  E  A  M  S  O  L  I  V  E  W  O  O  D
E  K  Z  F  J  G  Q  T  H  F  Z  F  C  A  Q  S
V  O  Y  F  J  P  W  V  X  R  L  H  J  A  A  R
O  F  S  D  O  D  S  D  A  G  E  O  S  P  A  Q
H  T  M  T  S  G  I  T  S  R  O  F  G  D  T  C
S  H  S  S  N  L  L  A  U  D  A  L  E  R  D  Y
C  E  E  I  O  A  E  B  L  E  N  C  D  H  O  P
A  C  W  L  C  L  S  E  S  R  Q  A  Q  N  O  R
R  O  O  W  Q  T  O  Y  H  Q  E  P  T  H  R  E
V  V  L  X  O  Q  J  M  C  W  C  V  I  S  P  S
I  E  Q  N  E  V  P  D  O  K  K  R  O  O  O  S
N  N  E  K  H  N  S  Q  H  N  A  G  Z  W  S  E
G  A  L  J  A  U  L  A  M  M  L  O  U  C  T  Y
S  N  J  T  S  E  E  R  T  M  L  A  P  J  S  B
P  T  N  X  P  O  M  E  G  R  A  N  A  T  E  S
```

Good Old Moses ∾∾∾∾∾∾∾∾∾∾∾∾∾∾∾∾∾∾∾∾∾∾∾∾∾∾∾∾∾

In this word search, attempt to find 25 entries associated with Moses. Answers on page 69.

```
A D B A S K E T Y S E I P S F P
O L W C O M M A N D M E N T S H
V H V Z F A D S S A J F H E N O
W F S A S S U H E E A C A P H A
A A G U T E E H T U M R R N P R
N P E A B P T H S I G O O H A A
D O F S H G R I R O M A T N S H
E F S E D O N I L I J R L W S P
R W R U Q E A I S E E C U P O T
J D Y B D M R E N S A Q T U V R
K M V W E O D H E R J R X E E E
I A G T G L X D F T U Y S A R J
A N G M A I S E I C D B M I U R
N N Z N R F R Q U A I L S U R H
I A D N E B O Y R E V A L S U V
S Q K L E T M Y P E O P L E G O
```

Aaron	Israelites	Nebo	Red Sea
Basket	Jethro	Passover	Shepherd
Burning Bush	Joshua	Pharaoh	Sinai
Command-ments	Let My People Go	Plagues	Slavery
		Promised Land	Spies
Desert	Manna		Staff
Exodus	Miriam	Quail	Wander

All 25 listed words have something to do with Daniel. Answers on page 69.

Abednego	Gold	Meshach	Vision
Angel	Hananiah	Nebuchad-nezzar	Wall
Clay	Jerusalem	Right	Wisdom
Daniel	Lions	Shadrach	Worship
Den	Magicians	Sorcerers	Writing
Dreams	Medes	Tekel	
Fire	Mene		

```
H  A  I  N  A  N  A  H  Q  N  S  M
O  W  J  E  R  U  S  A  L  E  M  L
T  I  K  B  M  O  E  R  L  S  A  W
A  S  J  U  E  G  D  I  E  H  E  O
O  D  S  C  S  E  E  G  I  A  R  R
W  O  N  H  H  N  M  H  N  D  D  S
W  M  A  A  A  D  O  T  A  R  L  H
R  N  I  D  C  E  G  I  D  A  O  I
I  O  C  N  H  B  F  N  L  C  G  P
T  I  I  E  S  A  E  G  E  H  C  T
I  S  G  Z  L  E  G  N  A  D  L  E
N  I  A  Z  W  A  L  L  E  C  A  K
G  V  M  A  B  F  I  R  E  M  Y  E
S  R  E  R  E  C  R  O  S  T  A  L
```

> *In this puzzle, find 25 entries associated with the fiery prophets*
> *Elijah and Elisha. Answers on page 69.*

```
K P N B W M O U N T C A R M E L S V
K D A W A N E A R T H Q U A K E L F
E E R I F F O T O I R A H C H Y Z N
C U H N Z J W O N C A K B W G E Z D
I G Y T M K B W A I X L H A K H E U
E E T W A E A R E J G I V L A D V G
C H C C R H T D Q L R A D M N L W N
N A K O L R P R E L E R P U Y T A V
E Z H C Y A A E W L O B O R A W D V
L I A T O T B I R U T R E H Q Y I X
I Z U X L N N R G A R N A Z S U C S
S F J A H D A H O U Z B A O E X H N
R I N G C E T A S O P D R M O J E E
E R T R R P A F M B M P M I F M R V
E E B F J G K D R A E T L S K U I A
H E J H S Q O B P L N B R O U I T R
S Z O U D A E H D L A B Z E Q B H C
S E T I M M A N U H S V P C E X O K
```

Ahab	Drought	Mantle	Surrounded
Altar	Earthquake	Mount Carmel	Wadi Cherith
Ax Head	Fire	Naaman	Whirlwind
Baal	Gehazi	Oil	Zarephath
Baldhead	Horeb	Ravens	
Broom Tree	Jezebel	Sheer Silence	
Chariot of Fire	Leprosy	Shunammite	

This puzzle has 25 entries associated with that daring biblical heroine, Ruth. Search for them all. Answers on page 69.

Barley	Feet	Mother-in-Law	Sandal
Bethlehem	Glean	My God	Threshing Floor
Blessed	Grain	Naomi	
Boaz	Kinsman	Obed	Winnow
Chilion	Mahlon	Orpah	Your People
Elimelech	Mara	Reapers	
Famine	Moab	Redeem	

```
W  O  N  N  I  W  B  B  N  Z  A  O  B  W  L
S  R  E  P  A  E  R  L  O  A  R  A  M  T  A
K  K  X  B  I  D  G  M  I  O  Y  B  D  H  D
H  M  B  L  A  R  V  A  L  V  N  A  K  R  N
E  M  L  B  A  O  H  H  I  Q  A  R  F  E  A
L  F  E  I  E  A  M  L  H  O  M  L  A  S  S
P  E  N  E  P  T  I  O  C  Y  S  E  O  H  E
O  L  T  R  D  M  H  N  N  M  N  Y  W  I  B
E  I  O  E  O  E  N  L  Y  Y  I  P  Q  N  L
P  M  O  A  E  A  R  G  E  V  K  D  J  G  E
R  E  N  I  E  F  O  Q  J  H  E  V  G  F  S
U  L  L  L  N  D  T  M  Z  B  E  M  M  L  S
O  E  G  P  Y  D  E  R  O  E  Y  M  I  O  E
Y  C  M  O  T  H  E  R  I  N  L  A  W  O  D
A  H  K  E  N  I  M  A  F  Z  J  O  X  R  I
```

Jumping Jehoshaphat!

> *J is a popular first letter for Bible names and other significant words. There are 25 J words here. Can you find them? Answers on page 69.*

```
A  S  W  E  J  E  N  D  G  A  H  A  E  S
E  C  M  I  H  A  O  U  K  C  P  C  L  U
C  I  V  J  Q  S  T  J  F  G  E  O  S  J
I  R  O  A  L  N  A  O  F  D  S  J  S  E
T  J  H  E  M  O  H  S  J  I  O  U  A  R
S  U  W  S  D  J  P  I  J  S  J  D  D  U
U  E  W  L  O  U  A  A  O  S  B  G  U  S
J  J  J  K  J  D  H  H  R  U  D  M  J  A
N  O  P  R  O  E  S  D  C  J  F  E  E  L
B  S  N  J  E  P  O  A  T  G  R  N  S  E
J  E  S  A  L  W  H  E  S  E  H  T  U  M
O  G  T  C  T  B  E  F  M  Y  L  J  S  H
S  D  U  O  X  H  J  I  H  I  O  Z  O  A
H  U  V  B  C  H  A  V  O  H  E  J  Q  D
U  J  O  N  A  H  E  N  N  J  A  Y  M  U
A  W  S  U  R  I  A  J  O  R  D  A  N  J
```

Jacob	Jewels	Jordan	Jude
Jairus	Jews	Joseph	Judges
Jehoshaphat	Job	Joshua	Judgment
Jehovah	Joel	Josiah	Justice
Jeremiah	John	Joy	
Jerusalem	Jonah	Judah	
Jesus	Jonathan	Judas	

..

The Experience Was in Tents

As they wandered in the wilderness, the Israelites worshiped God in a Tabernacle, a tent-based complex. Exodus 35–40 offers detailed instructions about the construction of this portable sanctuary. You'll find 25 key terms in this puzzle. Answers on page 69.

```
W  O  K  R  I  A  H  S  T  A  O  G  Q  O  A  I
X  A  D  N  A  T  S  P  M  A  L  D  G  O  C  N
Q  S  H  G  Z  U  M  C  Y  K  I  L  N  Q  A  I
S  P  N  E  S  A  A  A  O  P  R  M  I  X  C  G
O  T  E  I  L  L  R  D  S  U  I  A  T  N  I  E
T  F  N  T  A  N  W  A  O  B  R  M  E  G  A  M
G  H  A  E  S  T  L  O  U  H  L  T  E  F  Q  B
N  R  S  L  M  C  R  R  B  I  P  U  M  S  S  R
I  S  O  E  Y  T  E  U  N  V  E  E  F  K  T  O
R  S  N  T  M  H  S  E  C  B  S  X  O  I  I  I
E  I  X  I  C  A  N  E  R  O  O  A  T  A  B  D
V  L  Y  M  S  T  R  O  V  J  W  V  N  W  U  E
O  V  Q  K  A  A  N  F  Q  I  M  Y  E  T  C  R
C  E  Z  B  V  Z  B  C  D  F  D  Y  T  Y  D  E
O  R  L  D  E  T  A  E  S  Y  C  R  E  M  U  D
U  E  P  H  O  L  Y  T  O  T  H  E  L  O  R  D
```

Acacia	Clasp	Frames	Silver
Altar	Court	Goats' Hair	Table
Ark	Covering	Holy to the Lord	Tent of Meeting
Basins	Cubits		
Bowls	Curtains	Lampstand	Vestments
Bronze	Embroidered	Linen	Yarns
Cherubim	Ephod	Mercy Seat	

Singer Slinger

In this puzzle, find 25 words associated with David. Answers on page 70.

Abigail	Goliath	Michal	Shepherd
Absalom	Jesse	Mighty	Sling
Bathsheba	Jonathan	Music	Solomon
Bear	King	Nathan	Ziklag
Bethlehem	Lion	Philistines	
Brothers	Lyre	Psalms	
Cave	Mephibosheth	Saul	

```
E  S  S  E  J  J  O  N  A  T  H  A  N  G  X  K
V  K  H  T  E  H  S  O  B  I  H  P  E  M  L  X
Z  O  Y  N  V  G  S  O  W  R  I  R  U  Z  Y  K
U  D  L  K  E  A  P  U  D  W  B  M  G  H  R  A
A  R  D  Z  U  H  Q  P  W  C  U  O  T  D  E  T
B  E  B  L  A  S  E  N  I  T  S  I  L  I  H  P
E  H  R  E  A  B  C  N  M  B  J  E  C  Y  B  N
H  P  G  U  T  N  I  O  A  S  G  S  M  X  R  O
S  E  M  A  O  H  L  G  M  T  L  R  L  F  O  H
H  H  C  I  L  A  L  L  A  I  H  A  M  K  T  T
T  S  L  I  S  K  A  E  N  I  H  A  I  L  H  A
A  C  Y  B  S  S  I  G  H  C  L  N  N  C  E  I
B  A  A  P  P  U  V  Z  I  E  G  U  R  T  R  L
Y  V  Y  B  R  K  M  M  C  F  M  I  C  B  S  O
H  E  M  N  O  M  O  L  O  S  Q  S  W  N  R  G
P  T  P  Q  Y  T  H  G  I  M  R  A  E  B  O  N
```

Israel and Judah were ruled by many kings. Find 27 of those rulers in this word search. Answers on page 70.

```
H  J  B  Y  Z  M  A  O  B  O  H  E  R  A
A  M  A  R  O  H  E  J  O  A  S  H  T  Z
I  M  H  S  M  J  E  H  O  I  A  K  I  M
L  A  A  E  J  R  N  A  D  A  B  S  L  B
A  J  E  H  O  S  H  A  P  H  A  T  H  N
H  I  H  B  T  Q  J  R  Z  A  P  O  M  A
T  B  O  J  H  D  O  U  I  I  R  M  O  H
A  A  S  E  A  A  S  R  H  K  O  A  W  A
M  B  H  H  M  U  I  L  D  E  O  N  H  Z
A  Z  E  O  A  Z  A  K  S  D  J  A  A  I
Z  A  A  A  M  Y  H  I  E  E  N  S  L  A
I  H  O  H  H  A  I  R  A  Z  A  S  E  H
A  A  Z  A  M  O  N  M  O  L  E  E  L  A
H  T  M  Z  E  C  H  A  R  I  A  H  F  S
```

Abijam	Baasha	Jeroboam
Ahab	Elah	Joash
Ahaz	Hezekiah	Josiah
Ahaziah	Hoshea	Jotham
Amaziah	Jehoahaz	Manasseh
Amon	Jehoiakim	Nadab
Asa	Jehoram	Rehoboam
Athaliah	Jehoshaphat	Zechariah
Azariah	Jehu	Zedekiah

Not Your Average Joe ഇഇഇഇഇഇഇഇഇഇഇഇഇഇഇഇഇഇ

It's clear from the Book of Genesis that Joseph was not very ordinary. Attacked, enslaved, imprisoned—he kept rising to the top. This puzzle has 28 words and names from Joseph's story. Answers on page 70.

```
T Z D G S R E H T O R B R W V
N I M A J N E B M M T I P K V
F K I J B N S R N S T I D V R
G P B T A T E A S C X R G E L
G O T T D C V B O H E G R R N
O T K F P A O V U A E A A I I
O I F E R Y E B M E E A N N A
D P S A P R G D E B R Y V G R
L H C S S C O E P B S L B E G
O A M E E T O U P R O F A D S
O R E O H I C W A R J R K O N
K R W A O K P T S R I K E O I
I N N Y R N S S L L W S R L L
N U W B D H O A R A H P O B E
G S Q R S I L V E R C U P N X
```

Baker	Dream	Pharaoh	Silver Cup
Benjamin	Egypt	Pit	Spies
Blood	Good-looking	Potiphar	Stars
Brothers	Grain	Prison	Sun
Caravan	Jacob	Reuben	
Cows	Moon	Ring	
Cupbearer	Nile	Robe	
Dothan	Overseer	Sheaves	

Jesus had a family tree. We get two views of it, in Matthew 1:1–16 and Luke 3:23–38. There are 25 of his best-known ancestors squeezed into the trunk and branches of this tree. Can you find them all? Answers on page 70.

```
E U F        K G M        N Q M        H A R M P
E U J W      V V K        O M N        M G C A D
N P Q S T    S F F        W F U B      C N X A R
N L N C H Q  D H M F      N G K D    Z J L B G Y
    V H R T F J L E R     R C T J  X A V R E
      L A X H G U U M     X A U P J C I A
        P I K E T D P     H S H A O W H
          A S H X I A P H H E B E A     R V U W
I B Y       F O Q E A H P J D N M       U E H Z
V N A H     G J H B E M I D I O     Z Z C V
Y H V H S   F S J S A E Z I I I C Z I A Q
    A C A Z O L O X P T D N P V I H A Z
      I T R H T J S H O H B N H A A S D
      K E L M A L N L U H O H V I D
      J E W E V M Z Y S T P A H D
        C Z R B H A N A E Q A Z
        L E K A M R L S O D J
        D H A B C E N Y E H
        U D F R B H W S V R
        A R B Z H U S Y D N
        Y L N Z V E R E K A
        W W F J R I P E F I
        S L X X O L N S Z J
        N M A O B O H E R E
        I N O M O L O S C X
```

Abraham	Jacob	Mary	Seth
Adam	Jehoshaphat	Methusaleh	Shem
Boaz	Jesse	Noah	Solomon
David	Joseph	Rahab	Tamar
Enoch	Josiah	Rehoboam	Uzziah
Hezekiah	Judah	Ruth	Zerubbabel
Isaac			

Earthly Stories with Heavenly Meanings

Jesus taught many truths by using parables. Find the 28 parable-related words in the puzzle. Answers on page 70.

Banquet	Robbers	Tax Collector
Goats	Robe	Teaching
Hear	Rock	Tenants
Love	Samaritan	Treasure
Mustard	Sand	Vineyard
Neighbor	Seeds	Wedding
Pearl	Sheep	Weeds
Pharisee	Shepherd	Wheat
Prodigal	Sons	
Rich	Sower	

```
A  P  K  S  H  E  E  P  G  D  Z  R  E  W  O  S
R  E  T  C  O  G  R  O  B  H  G  I  E  N  A  H
T  A  X  C  O  L  L  E  C  T  O  R  B  M  R  E
P  R  Q  A  B  R  C  W  S  N  A  T  A  T  O  P
L  L  T  U  S  D  E  E  W  E  R  R  N  E  B  H
O  S  R  O  B  E  F  D  H  D  I  E  Q  N  B  E
V  I  N  E  Y  A  R  D  E  T  C  A  U  A  E  R
E  S  S  A  N  D  G  I  A  T  H  S  E  N  R  D
D  R  A  T  S  U  M  N  T  L  M  U  T  T  S  K
T  E  A  C  H  I  N  G  P  H  A  R  I  S  E  E
P  R  O  D  I  G  A  L  S  D  E  E  S  H  J  F
```

Familiar Christmas words are the subject of this word search. There are 28 entries to find. Answers on page 70.

```
L  E  G  N  A  E  D  U  J  E  S  U  S
I  S  F  I  R  S  T  B  O  R  N  D  W
N  D  R  H  E  R  O  D  S  M  A  S  I
N  R  A  E  A  S  T  O  E  E  U  T  S
M  E  N  E  G  Y  N  H  P  S  G  A  E
A  H  K  J  O  I  E  F  H  S  U  R  M
E  P  I  J  H  L  S  R  G  I  S  E  E
R  E  N  K  H  P  R  T  C  A  T  G  N
D  H  C  T  O  Y  T  Y  E  H  U  N  H
L  S  E  L  M  S  R  U  B  R  S  A  T
E  B  N  A  Z  A  R  E  T  H  E  M  O
I  M  S  N  M  Q  R  A  G  O  L  D  L
F  E  E  L  I  L  A  G  I  F  T  S  C
```

Angel	First Born	Jesus	Myrrh
Augustus	Frankincense	Joseph	Nazareth
Bethlehem	Galilee	Judea	Registered
Cloth	Gifts	Joy	Shepherds
Dream	Gold	Manger	Son
East	Herod	Mary	Star
Field	Inn	Messiah	Wise Men

Super S's

Many words in the Bible begin with the letter S. Twenty-eight of them are in this puzzle. Answers on page 71.

```
S  T  N  I  A  S  U  F  F  E  R  I  N  G  M  S
M  O  D  O  S  A  P  E  E  H  S  A  S  I  G  A
L  U  A  S  T  V  N  I  S  S  I  N  G  N  A  B
S  A  N  C  T  I  F  I  C  A  T  I  O  N  E  B
C  Y  G  R  L  O  G  R  S  R  Z  S  X  A  S  A
R  O  N  N  S  R  D  O  P  U  M  H  M  T  A  T
I  N  S  A  L  V  A  T  I  O  N  E  E  I  C  H
P  O  I  B  G  S  O  W  R  L  F  P  X  R  R  L
T  S  M  A  L  O  S  A  I  W  H  H  N  A  E  E
U  M  E  S  T  R  G  V  T  E  P  E  Q  M  D  U
R  A  O  U  A  E  L  U  N  G  Y  R  E  A  C  M
E  S  N  T  N  A  V  R  E  S  P  D  H  S  R  A
S  T  S  I  M  O  N  E  C  I  F  I  R  C  A  S
```

Sabbath	Samuel	Shepherd	Song
Sacred	Sanctification	Simeon	Spirit
Sacrifice	Saul	Simon	Star
Saints	Savior	Sin	Stephen
Salvation	Scriptures	Sinai	Suffering
Samaritan	Servant	Sing	Sun
Samson	Sheep	Sodom	Synagogue

The Floating Zoo

Aboard this boat are 30 things and people from the story of Noah and the ark in Genesis 6–9. Answers on page 71.

Altar	Cubits	Forty Days	Righteous
Animals	Cypress	Ham	Roof
Ararat	Decks	Japheth	Shem
Ark	Door	Noah	Two
Birds	Dove	Olive Leaf	Violence
Bow	Favor	Pitch	Waters
Covenant	Floated	Rain	
Creeping Things	Flood	Raven	

```
            H S Y A D Y T R O F D A
            C S O L I V E L E A F R
            N N Q I X     N C Y M A
            R E C T E     J O U F R
            C V R A D E T A O L F A
            W A E P L R S D R I B T
N K T D N R E N V I O L E N C E O R R Q
S W R O K E P B C V S R P F E K W R A Y
O T A A H A I O I O O S A A J V I V T F
S H I U O M N W T O V V E A E G O X L S
B K M B E A G N F P O E P R H L B D A
  W C H U E T H I R P H N T P S F N C
    S E Z C H S V A E I E A L Y K O
    A K D X I R R T R O T A N F C H
      V O W N D H E U S M C L T A
        I W G Z O S T I P O H M
          S G M O N A O A
          B J A R D W
```

The Gospel Truth

This puzzle bears the names of 30 people mentioned in the Gospels of Matthew, Mark, Luke, and John. Answers on page 71.

Andrew
Anna
Bartholomew
Bartimaeus
Caiaphas
Elizabeth
Herod
Jairus

James
Jesus
John
Joseph
Judas Iscariot
Lazarus
Mark
Martha

Mary
Mary Magdalene
Matthew
Nathanael
Nicodemus
Peter
Philip

Pontius Pilate
Simeon
Simon
Thomas
Zacchaeus
Zebedee
Zechariah

P	D	F	B	A	R	T	H	O	L	O	M	E	W	M	T
L	E	A	N	A	H	T	A	N	A	N	N	A	S	A	O
J	L	I	N	U	E	G	S	G	S	S	H	U	M	R	I
O	R	E	T	E	P	L	J	I	A	E	R	Y	S	Y	R
E	E	D	E	B	E	Z	I	H	M	I	M	U	W	M	A
N	S	S	D	M	W	P	Z	A	E	S	A	S	A	C	
I	U	E	U	A	S	A	E	J	A	E	O	U	J	G	S
C	E	H	R	H	I	U	P	R	J	B	E	N	P	D	I
O	A	K	P	A	Y	I	R	A	D	A	E	M	J	A	S
D	M	D	C	E	L	R	H	A	H	N	A	T	S	L	A
E	I	V	O	I	S	T	A	C	Z	T	A	I	H	E	D
M	T	I	H	R	R	O	C	M	T	A	M	N	O	N	U
U	R	P	Q	A	E	A	J	H	Y	O	L	Y	X	E	J
S	A	B	M	M	Z	H	E	E	N	S	A	M	O	H	T
A	B	J	O	H	N	W	Z	E	C	H	A	R	I	A	H
P	E	T	A	L	I	P	S	U	I	T	N	O	P	N	H

In this puzzle, can you find the names of 30 people associated with the early church (the Book of Acts and the Epistles)? Answers on page 71.

```
P  I  X  F  E  L  I  X  L  Y  D  I  A  M  S  Z
I  S  I  O  L  S  A  I  H  T  T  A  M  I  U  S
L  S  N  A  E  P  O  N  D  L  A  Q  M  U  I  A
I  X  O  G  R  X  G  O  E  L  U  Y  H  U  L  L
H  R  I  L  E  I  R  T  I  H  I  A  P  V  E  I
P  T  S  K  L  E  H  U  I  F  P  H  P  E  N  S
E  R  T  U  H  O  Q  P  E  M  O  E  S  W  R  S
C  P  E  S  I  A  P  S  P  E  O  A  T  E  O  S
N  R  L  T  N  R  T  A  B  A  B  T  C  S  C  A
N  I  M  Z  E  U  T  E  A  A  S  I  H  L  I  I
U  S  O  A  S  P  J  E  N  D  N  Y  U  Y  S  N
E  C  F  T  R  N  U  R  M  R  O  A  E  R  E  A
P  I  C  S  V  Y  A  C  E  E  S  H  C  N  M  N
E  L  T  B  C  B  L  B  K  A  D  N  R  F  A  A
A  L  E  M  P  E  R  O  R  L  U  K  E  V  J  R
U  A  J  O  H  N  A  G  R  I  P  P  A  C  D  K
```

Agrippa	Emperor	Lydia	Priscilla
Ananias	Felix	Mary	Rhoda
Apollos	Festus	Matthias	Sapphira
Aquila	Herod	Paul	Saul
Barnabas	James	Peter	Silas
Bernice	John	Philip	Stephen
Cornelius	Lois	Phoebe	Timothy
Demetrius	Luke		

Eat, Drink, and Be Satisfied

No strange foods here—this could be a shopping list taken to a modern food store! Search for these 31 delicious foods. Answers on page 71.

Almond	Corn	Honey	Onion
Apple	Cucumber	Lamb	Pomegranate
Barley	Egg	Leek	Quail
Bean	Fig	Lentil	Raisin
Bread	Fish	Melon	Salt
Cake	Goat	Milk	Wheat
Calf	Grape	Mustard	Wine
Cheese	Herbs	Olive	

```
K  L  I  M  G  R  A  P  E  P  D  N  L
R  A  I  S  I  N  R  O  R  U  A  C  E
E  O  V  F  I  S  H  M  N  E  F  E  N
K  O  L  I  V  E  Q  E  B  I  S  H  T
A  A  Q  H  T  A  O  G  G  L  O  O  I
C  U  C  U  M  B  E  R  S  I  T  N  L
L  B  D  N  O  M  L  A  C  A  M  E  E
E  B  A  B  M  A  L  N  W  U  E  Y  G
E  A  E  H  A  T  X  A  S  Q  L  B  W
K  R  R  C  B  O  P  T  B  K  O  I  M
O  L  B  Z  O  P  A  E  R  Y  N  K  E
J  E  P  N  L  R  E  S  E  E  H  C  G
A  Y  M  E  D  L  N  W  H  E  A  T  G
```

> *One of the best-loved portions of Scripture is the twenty-third Psalm. This word search contains 31 key words from those 6 verses. Can you find them all? Answers on page 71.*

```
R  A  E  F  C  B  S  H  T  A  P  I  V  T  B  T
R  S  S  E  N  S  U  Y  X  T  H  G  I  R  W  A
F  K  X  Y  H  C  G  Z  T  G  C  K  X  N  A  B
L  D  Z  E  Q  R  U  W  J  W  S  J  Y  H  L  L
L  O  A  I  E  W  A  P  M  D  W  O  O  U  K  E
I  D  T  E  G  T  E  E  W  A  W  U  U  V  S  C
T  S  N  R  E  O  R  R  N  O  S  E  S  L  H  E
S  L  E  R  O  C  O  T  A  E  L  E  K  S  E  K
V  W  S  I  Y  F  S  D  F  P  R  L  Y  L  P  T
A  E  L  Z  M  T  M  E  N  U  E  A  O  B  H  N
L  D  O  L  A  E  R  O  T  E  D  R  L  F  E  I
L  A  R  F  E  W  N  S  C  C  S  O  P  O  R  O
E  S  F  O  V  W  A  E  A  Q  R  S  I  V  D  N
Y  S  Q  E  D  P  D  U  S  D  V  L  A  O  N  A
D  N  R  S  E  R  O  T  S  E  R  K  M  L  U  F
Q  H  T  M  E  D  O  P  R  E  S  E  N  C  E  X
```

Anoint	Goodness	Paths	Staff
Comfort	Green	Prepare	Still
Cup	Head	Presence	Table
Days	House	Restores	Valley
Dwell	Lord	Right	Walk
Enemies	Mercy	Rod	Want
Fear	Oil	Shepherd	Waters
Follow	Pastures	Soul	

Awesome Happenings

The 32 words in this puzzle are found in the accounts of Jesus' miracles. Answers on page 72.

Alive	Eyes	Peter
Bed	Fish	Pool
Blind	Girl	Restored
Bread	Hand	Servant
Centurion	Hear	Storm
Clean	Jairus	Walked
Coin	Lazarus	Water
Crippled	Lepers	Waves
Dead	Mute	Wind
Deaf	Nain	Withered
Demons	Paralyzed	

```
D  P  O  O  L  M  O  B  L  I  N  D  H
E  R  C  E  N  T  U  R  I  O  N  S  E
M  N  R  P  Q  N  S  T  O  R  M  T  A
O  S  I  L  F  M  H  K  E  D  D  C  R
N  R  P  A  R  A  L  Y  Z  E  D  O  S
S  E  P  H  N  J  E  E  A  K  D  I  E
L  P  L  D  G  S  F  D  D  L  N  N  V
R  E  E  W  A  T  E  R  C  A  I  A  A
I  L  D  E  R  E  H  T  I  W  W  L  W
G  R  E  S  T  O  R  E  D  H  S  I  F
C  L  E  A  N  P  R  E  T  E  P  V  B
J  A  I  R  U  S  D  A  E  R  B  E  A
T  N  A  V  R  E  S  U  R  A  Z  A  L
```

Abraham, Isaac, and Jacob are the spiritual ancestors of every believer. In the following puzzle are 33 words associated with our three "dads." Answers on page 72.

E	L	M	E	L	C	H	I	Z	E	D	E	K	C	G	N
L	E	E	C	I	F	I	R	C	A	S	F	O	L	T	R
I	A	I	B	Q	U	J	D	C	S	H	M	L	T	N	A
E	H	B	B	I	M	P	U	G	H	O	I	T	O	A	C
Z	I	N	L	T	R	A	R	A	T	V	D	G	L	N	H
E	S	A	E	N	S	T	G	E	E	W	I	O	S	E	E
R	H	B	S	E	A	A	H	S	B	E	E	L	M	V	L
R	M	A	S	Z	R	A	T	R	N	E	E	L	W	O	S
E	A	L	I	R	S	O	N	I	I	M	K	D	V	C	A
T	E	I	N	V	C	G	M	A	A	G	B	A	P	E	R
H	L	Z	G	K	M	A	N	C	C	L	H	E	H	L	A
G	N	T	J	M	F	O	E	I	I	Y	E	T	T	E	H
U	A	O	W	K	M	I	R	N	K	H	S	E	H	G	L
A	R	W	W	G	S	H	D	I	S	W	N	T	P	N	E
L	A	W	W	E	L	L	S	P	A	T	X	A	E	A	E
G	H	S	R	O	T	I	S	I	V	H	S	E	T	W	H

Angel	Famine	Livestock	Sheep
Birthright	Hagar	Lot	Sodom
Blessing	Haran	Melchizedek	Stew
Blind	Heel	Moriah	Tent
Camels	Ishmael	Rachel	Twelve
Canaan	Kings	Rebekah	Visitors
Covenant	Laban	Sacrifice	Wells
Eliezer	Laughter	Sarah	
Esau	Leah		

> **There are 35 names of people from the Book of Genesis hidden in this puzzle. How many can you find? Answers on page 72.**

```
Y  H  U  N  I  L  A  T  H  P  A  N  K  J  J  H
L  P  K  G  I  B  E  N  J  A  M  I  N  H  B  A
A  E  Z  V  G  A  L  E  B  A  K  L  A  G  M  G
B  S  H  A  O  N  C  S  D  M  U  R  E  A  J  A
A  O  W  M  A  E  H  H  A  I  A  A  H  A  N  R
N  J  Y  E  O  E  Q  D  A  S  N  A  S  F  H  H
Y  P  N  L  M  L  A  B  L  K  R  A  W  E  P  E
G  O  U  C  K  E  H  O  O  B  E  I  H  R  H  L
B  T  N  H  Z  A  T  K  A  C  S  B  A  O  A  A
R  I  R  I  J  M  V  F  C  S  A  C  E  E  R  S
E  P  L  Z  U  H  M  L  A  A  H  J  N  R  A  U
U  H  G  E  D  S  O  C  E  E  A  O  P  Q  O  H
B  A  J  D  A  I  H  B  L  V  C  S  U  A  H  T
E  R  I  E  H  A  H  A  M  H  I  B  I  S  E  E
N  C  Y  K  R  J  A  P  H  E  T  H  U  Z  V  M
D  O  R  E  H  S  A  N  U  L  U  B  E  Z  E  B
```

Abel	Eve	Judah	Pharaoh
Abraham	Hagar	Laban	Potiphar
Adam	Ham	Leah	Rachel
Asher	Isaac	Levi	Rebekah
Benjamin	Ishmael	Lot	Reuben
Cain	Issachar	Melchizedek	Sarah
Dinah	Jacob	Methusaleh	Shem
Enoch	Japheth	Naphtali	Zebulun
Esau	Joseph	Noah	

There were 12 original tribes of Israel. Find the tribes and related words in this puzzle. After you have found all 17 words, unscramble the leftover letters to reveal the mystery word. Answers on page 72.

Asher

Benjamin

Canaan

Clans

Dan

Ephraim

Gad

Issachar

Joseph

Judah

Levi

Manasseh

Naphtali

Reuben

Simeon

Territory

Zebulun

```
Y  M  B  E  N  J  A  M  I  N
R  A  N  P  J  N  U  V  S  N
O  N  E  H  O  U  E  D  S  A
T  A  B  R  S  L  S  T  A  P
I  S  U  A  E  U  E  S  C  H
R  S  E  I  P  B  H  I  H  T
R  E  R  M  H  E  E  M  A  A
E  H  P  G  R  Z  A  E  R  L
T  C  A  N  A  A  N  O  L  I
S  N  A  L  C  D  A  N  I  N
```

_ _ _ _ _ _ _

Getting from Here to There ∽∽∽∽∽∽∽∽∽∽∽∽∽∽∽∽∽∽∽∽∽

Traveling in Bible times was slow and often quite difficult. First unscramble the words, and then find the 15 entries in the word search. Answers on page 72.

ACELM _ _ _ _ _

TRAC _ _ _ _

OHTRIAC _ _ _ _ _ _ _

TOLC _ _ _ _

OEYNKD _ _ _ _ _ _

SRHEO _ _ _ _ _

LEUM _ _ _ _

NEOX _ _ _ _

TARF _ _ _ _

WRO SBOTA _ _ _
_ _ _ _ _

NNNIRUG _ _ _ _ _ _ _

LASI TSAOB _ _ _ _ _
_ _ _ _ _

SSPHI _ _ _ _ _

GANWO _ _ _ _ _ _

GWNLAIK _ _ _ _ _ _ _ _

```
B  G  J  M  U  L  E  D
W  A  L  K  I  N  G  L
S  H  I  P  S  D  C  F
A  W  O  X  C  O  I  S
I  A  R  R  L  N  M  T
L  G  A  T  S  K  L  A
B  O  F  T  N  E  E  O
O  N  T  E  R  Y  M  B
A  E  X  A  H  A  A  W
T  O  I  R  A  H  C  O
S  G  N  I  N  N  U  R
```

There are 14 words from the Beatitudes, Matthew 5:3–12, in this puzzle. After you find each word, write it below. If you find all 14 words correctly, the leftover letters will spell **Beatitude.** *Answers on page 73.*

```
K  T  B  T  S  R  I  H  T
P  I  G  L  A  D  N  B  M
R  R  N  E  E  E  O  E  P
O  I  A  G  V  S  R  G  O
P  P  T  A  D  C  S  I  O
H  S  E  C  I  O  J  E  R
E  H  T  F  U  D  M  E  D
T  H  U  N  G  E  R  U  P
S  L  I  N  H  E  R  I  T
```

_ _ _ _ _ _   _ _ _ _ _ _ _

_ _ _ _   _ _ _ _

_ _ _   _ _ _ _ _ _ _ _

_ _ _ _ _ _   _ _ _ _

_ _ _ _ _ _   _ _ _ _ _ _ _

_ _ _ _ _ _ _   _ _ _ _ _ _

_ _ _ _ _ _ _   _ _ _ _ _ _

Top Ten List

The Ten Commandments are among the best-known verses of Scripture (Exodus 20:1–17). Can you fill in the blanks, and then find the 15 hidden words? Answers on page 73.

You shall have no other g_ _ _ before me.

You shall not make for yourself an i_ _ _.

You shall not make wrongful use of the n_ _ _ of the Lord.

R_ _ _ _ _ _ _ the s_ _ _ _ _ _ day, and keep it h_ _ _.

H_ _ _ _ your f_ _ _ _ _ and your m_ _ _ _ _.

You shall not m_ _ _ _ _.

You shall not commit a_ _ _ _ _ _ _.

You shall not s_ _ _ _ _.

You shall not bear f_ _ _ _ w_ _ _ _ _ _ against your neighbor.

You shall not c_ _ _ _ your neighbor's house... or anything that belongs to your neighbor.

```
            Z  Y  L                    X  X  L
         G  S  V  P  X              L  A  E  T  S
      L  Z  L  U  X  S  L        R  T  T  W  E  J  U
   R  D  G  X  I  O  D  S  O  K  L  S  D  O  G  Q  G  D
   Y  E  F  K  D  A  A  V  Z  Z  G  N  W  D  G  W  R  Z
   Y  L  D  A  V  B  D  W  L  B  A  I  A  J  W  K  M  D
   O  K  L  R  B  I  O  U  P  P  T  Y  W  M  G  D  E  Z
   X  N  R  A  U  C  D  F  L  N  O  S  L  Q  E  G  H  A
   E  Z  T  O  B  M  A  O  E  T  H  P  V  T  U  B  R  C
   A  H  V  N  N  D  V  S  L  O  E  X  A  Y  W  N  E  F
   L  I  R  M  Q  O  S  R  L  E  X  R  T  Y  G  D  B  V
   V  R  S  V  Y  E  H  Y  E  X  W  Z  Y  Q  V  H  M  O
   U  E  Y  J  E  J  D  K  U  H  Y  R  E  I  V  S  E  G
   W  H  G  R  A  R  Q  G        T  T  K  I  I  L  M  R
   L  T  F  N  R  G  T  F        L  O  T  W  M  U  E  Q
   L  A  B  M  U  Q  T  Q        Z  J  M  H  T  I  R  O
   F  F  R  C  O  V  E  T        E  S  L  A  F  E  N  J
```

Jesus Was Here

> *Here is a list of 16 cities Jesus visited. Fill in the missing vowels (a, e, i, o, u), and then solve the puzzle. Answers on page 73.*

```
A  N  A  C  O  T  Y  R  E  L
U  O  N  A  I  N  Y  E  V  O
M  A  G  D  A  L  A  D  E  T
B  E  T  H  L  E  H  E  M  N
N  S  T  N  I  Z  A  R  O  K
I  E  M  M  I  N  R  H  E  C
B  E  T  H  S  A  I  D  A  L
E  A  E  R  H  Z  E  P  L  O
T  Z  J  C  A  A  E  E  S  H
H  B  Y  R  R  R  T  L  U  C
P  S  S  A  N  E  R  E  A  I
H  N  B  A  D  T  C  N  M  R
A  A  U  G  O  H  A  T  M  E
G  M  E  L  A  S  U  R  E  J
E  C  A  E  S  A  R  E  A  C
```

B__th__ny   J__r__ch__
B__thl__h__m   J__r__s__l__m
B__thph__g__   K__r__z__n
B__ths____d__   M__gd__l__
C____s__r____   N____n
C__n__   N__z__r__th
C__p__rn____m   Sych__r
__mm____s   Tyr__

Bible Word Search Puzzles ⚫ 41

God's Daughters

```
E  D  E  B  O  R  A  H  B  H
I  V  O  R  A  C  H  E  L  T
B  L  E  R  E  H  T  S  E  E
P  R  I  S  C  I  L  L  A  B
M  E  N  I  M  A  C  E  I  A
A  B  H  A  R  A  S  A  D  Z
I  E  A  L  O  W  R  H  Y  I
R  K  Y  R  A  M  O  T  L  L
I  A  H  T  U  R  I  M  H  E
M  H  A  N  N  A  H  E  N  A
```

_ _ _ _ _ _ _   _ _ _ _ _

Deborah	Leah	Priscilla
Dorcas	Lydia	Rachel
Elizabeth	Martha	Rebekah
Esther	Mary	Ruth
Eve	Miriam	Sarah
Hannah	Naomi	

> There were many fathers and sons in the Bible. Some of those sons were fathers, and some of those fathers' sons were fathers. After you have found all 19 related words, the leftover letters will reveal the mystery word. Answers on page 74.

Abel	Delight	Jacob	Rehoboam
Abraham	Esau	Jesse	Seth
Adam	Honor	John	Solomon
Cain	Isaac	Joseph	Zechariah
David	Ishmael	Parent	

_ _ _ _ _ _ _ _

```
R  U  T  N  E  R  A  P  L  L
E  H  A  I  R  A  H  C  E  Z
H  T  J  S  B  J  P  A  B  C
O  E  O  D  E  O  M  B  A  A
B  S  S  A  S  H  C  R  D  I
O  R  E  V  S  N  A  A  T  N
A  O  P  I  E  R  M  H  J  I
M  N  H  D  J  C  A  A  S  I
A  O  R  S  O  L  O  M  O  N
C  H  H  D  E  L  I  G  H  T
```

> *This word square contains the names of all the books of the New Testament. Can you find them all without peeking at your Bible's table of contents? (Note: John, Corinthians, Thessalonians, Timothy, and Peter are listed once each. This means there are only 20 entries.) Answers on page 74.*

```
J K I P H I L E M O N X Y K M K
V P S W C O R I N T H I A N S V
J H I N M Y X E X U Y M J U G Q
A I P E A E H B P I H S W G S A
M L K J A I T T R E N S A D N Y
E I G F N I S O O A T L E P A F
S P T S T H M S I M A E N X I R
O P K U T A O S O T I V R O N E
K I S W N C E J I L K T T X O V
Y A J S O H A A Z R O R L W L E
E N A U P W N E A W O C Z B A L
K S A E D S Z M K C H C F J S A
U P F C D E D J P F L U K T S T
L J U F W K S S B H D O J V E I
L W E H T T A M E E Y R A B H O
A K A S W E R B E H W P B J T N
```

Twice the Lord asked Jonah to go to Nineveh. What happened as Jonah traveled? Use the letters to fill in the blanks in the list of 23 words from the Book of Jonah. Each letter will be used only once. Then find the words in the puzzle. Answers on page 74.

```
W  I  N  D  L  I  V  E  P  K  X  E  H
L  S  A  C  R  I  F  I  C  E  P  T  E
H  M  R  O  T  S  H  W  C  E  F  C  V
T  H  A  N  K  S  G  I  V  I  N  G  E
O  A  Y  R  G  N  A  O  E  A  B  C  N
L  M  R  O  W  V  L  F  R  J  U  H  I
C  Y  A  S  H  E  S  E  S  S  S  A  N
K  L  G  N  H  U  V  B  E  M  H  N  Y
C  L  C  B  K  I  N  G  A  P  P  O  J
A  E  C  A  L  G  S  A  R  H  Z  J  G
S  B  E  E  R  H  T  H  D  F  I  S  H
D  R  D  P  W  O  L  L  A  W  S  O  A
```

LETTERS

AA CCC D EEE FF GG HHHH III KK LLL MM
NN OOO PPP RRR SSS TT U V WWW

__n__ry	__i__h	Sac____lo__h	__arsh__sh
As__e__	J__na__	Sacri__i__e	T__anksg__v____ng
Be____y	Jo_____a	S_____	Th__e__
B__sh	__in__	__hi__	__in__
De__ive__an__e	L__v__	Sto_____	W__r__
E__il	__i__eva__	S__allo__	

Fairest in the Land

> **When you have found all 20 words in the puzzle, read the leftover letters from left to right, top to bottom. They will reveal the person who is the subject of this puzzle. Answers on page 75.**

```
Y  J  B  G  A  L  L  O  W  S  Q  C
O  E  A  E  V  A  S  H  T  I  R  U
J  W  N  I  A  C  E  D  R  O  M  K
C  S  Q  E  E  U  N  T  W  E  I  A
O  Q  U  E  E  N  T  N  O  N  R  I
U  R  E  S  S  T  H  I  G  L  U  S
S  A  T  S  A  V  E  E  F  R  P  R
I  D  S  A  H  S  U  E  R  U  S  E
N  A  M  A  H  A  N  G  E  D  L  P
```

— — — — — — — — —

Adar	Joy
Ahsuerus	King
Banquets	Mordecai
Beautiful	Persia
Cousin	Plot
Crown	Purim
Gallows	Queen
Haman	Save
Hanged	Susa
Jews	Vashti

Find the names of 21 biblical prophets in this puzzle, and write them below. Sixteen of them have books of the Old Testament named after them. You can find the others in these verses: 2 Samuel 7:2, 2 Kings 6:12, 2 Chronicles 21:12, Matthew 21:26, and Acts 11:27–28. Answers on page 75.

```
E R Q A Y N A H T A N W D A L
J S L Y A P T Z K E N M Q G J
O S O K F H X W I H W B Z A O
H O F E J A S A A O F E C B E
N M R H I E G I S E C H G U L
L A D H A G R I L H S W X S M
E H Q A A B S E A E W O I K A
I A Q H N A A R M H R W H D L
K J O U I I I K A I B Z D C A
E I H A F A E N K T A P D W C
Z L H N H P O L P U Q H D Q H
E E L A K J Y E E I K B G V I
B H W H K M I C A H H U S Y V
Z Z V U H A I D A B O J I Q H
U N R M L V Z E P H A N I A H
```

Busy B

These words begin with the letter **B**. *Make yourself busy by answering the 20 questions and then finding the words. Answers on page 75.*

1. City of Naomi, David, and a well-used stable (Ruth 1:1–2, 1 Samuel 17:12, Matthew 2)
B__ __ __ __ __ __ __ __

2. Where James and John were when Jesus called them (Matthew 4:21) B__ __ __

3. He saw the writing on the wall (Daniel 5)
B__ __ __ __ __ __ __ __ __

4. By the end of the story, he wasn't Ruthless anymore (Ruth 4:9–11) B__ __ __

5. What was the blind man doing as Jesus passed by him on his way to Jericho (Luke 18:35) B__ __ __ __ __ __

6. What the man was at the beginning of John 9, and the Pharisees were at the end
B__ __ __ __

7. Five units of this fed 5,000 (Matthew 15) B__ __ __ __

8. His name means "The Encourager," which he was for Paul and Mark (Acts 4:36)
B__ __ __ __ __ __ __

9. What God gave man (Genesis 2:7) B__ __ __ __ __

10. Joseph's baby brother (Genesis 35:24)
B__ __ __ __ __ __ __

11. Pilate released him instead of Jesus (Matthew 27:26)
B__ __ __ __ __ __ __

12. Us, if Jesus is the Vine (John 15:5) B__ __ __ __ __ __ __

13. City where they double-checked Paul's sermons (Acts 17:10–11) B__ __ __ __ __

14. He had a dream in prison, which Joseph interpreted (Genesis 40:16) B__ __ __ __

15. The wine of the Lord's Supper (Mark 14:24) B_ _ _ _

16. The captivating nation where the Jews "hung our harps" (Psalm 137:1–2) B_ _ _ _ _ _

17. The god who didn't rain on Elijah's parade (1 Kings 18) B_ _ _

18. What John did, when he wasn't eating locusts (Matthew 3) B_ _ _ _ _ _ _ _

19. Protrusion of Confusion (Genesis 11:9) B_ _ _ _ _

20. David killed one while defending his sheep (1 Samuel 17:35) B_ _ _

```
F H Z K J T C Z I A E O R E B B E A R L
L A A B D B C M P T N O L Y B A B E P D
G O Z L L T B U B E L R K B J J A N F K
O D Y I N L D R R Q B J E B A Q N M T B
B P N V O N E N L F Z O E K H J C E R H
F B G O H A R B I J Y G Y X A J H E H B
Z D D M A C R L B L G Z N R E B A E R O
G P R B E A W A O I B E A K R D Y E B S
S N D Z N H R J N R H P L O A E A T B A
M F I C O A E G H E N R T H B T B Y E B
M M H Z B N B L E Q I U P Q H U L E M A
N E I B I A J L H T E T I R O O U S H N
S Y A Z B T H A A T U F G L N X K U O R
S S Z E J T P V F J E V B E T B N H D A
L A L T E X H A Z Y O B I B F B O A T B
T H N B B P U H B A A V R C O D B B B P
B L T U M W Q R A Z Z A H S L E B E B H
C B E N J A M I N N F T L N T F U R B B
```

What's in a Name?

Bible people often went by two different names or had their names changed. First unscramble the changed name, and then find all 22 names in the word search. Answers on page 76.

ABRAM HAAARBM (Genesis 17:5) _ _ _ _ _ _ _

DANIEL RBELAZTEZASH (Daniel 1:7) _ _ _ - _ _ _ _ _ _ _ _

HADASSAH TRESHE (Esther 2:7) _ _ _ _ _ _

HANANIAH RDCHSHAA (Daniel 1:7) _ _ _ _ _ _ _ _

JACOB LESIAR (Genesis 32:28) _ _ _ _ _ _

LEVI TTMWEAH (Matthew 9:9 and Mark 2:14) _ _ _ _ _ _ _

MISHAEL HHMSEAC (Daniel 1:7) _ _ _ _ _ _ _

NATHANAEL WEMOLOHBTRA (John 1:45–49 and Matthew 10:3) _ _ _ _ _ _ _ _ - _ _ _ _

SARAI HAASR (Genesis 17:15) _ _ _ _ _

SAUL ULPA (Acts 13:9) _ _ _ _

SIMON TEERP (Matthew 4:18) _ _ _ _ _

R	E	H	T	S	E	J	D	A	N	I	E	L
A	B	R	A	H	A	M	Z	J	D	W	O	G
Z	M	H	C	A	H	S	E	M	E	E	L	P
Z	L	A	J	D	D	E	L	M	I	H	E	N
A	E	S	A	R	A	I	O	M	A	T	A	L
H	A	L	C	A	C	L	O	N	E	T	R	U
S	N	U	O	C	O	E	R	R	O	A	S	A
E	A	A	B	H	O	V	G	N	O	M	I	S
T	H	P	T	H	A	I	N	A	N	A	H	A
L	T	R	Z	M	A	R	B	A	Y	V	O	R
E	A	D	H	A	D	A	S	S	A	H	D	A
B	N	S	M	I	S	H	A	E	L	P	R	H

There are 22 words from 1 Corinthians 13 in this puzzle. Circle them, and write them below. Answers on page 76.

```
R  J  D  T  S  A  O  B  F  R  M  H
O  P  G  R  E  A  T  E  S  T  I  T
R  R  O  L  N  E  S  L  E  F  R  I
R  O  E  S  O  L  D  I  U  U  R  A
I  P  S  E  S  V  N  E  G  L  I  F
M  H  E  R  B  E  E  V  N  L  T  P
S  E  C  U  F  E  S  E  O  Y  A  A
L  C  I  D  D  A  A  S  T  T  B  B
E  I  O  N  E  N  C  R  I  R  L  I
G  E  J  E  P  T  I  E  S  O  E  D
N  S  E  K  O  N  N  K  E  A  N  E
A  E  R  A  H  T  R  U  T  H  J  S
```

The E's Have It

> **This word search has 21 words that begin with the letter E. First take the quiz to figure out what they are. Answers on page 76.**

```
P G H Z P S N P Y E L H S L E O Y G Z D
E B A M H F W E E R N J T E E X H A N R
F L E C T Y G B Q G I O S R J G H M J E
S Q I J E T U R H E Y V C U A P C X T W
H N M J B U X Q E I T P M H I E U F F E
T G E R A T W P V M E K T L G B C Z E C
L J J E Z H E Y E T C X E S U C I X I C
Z M M U I R L E D S C X Q S U A N L C M
G E L E L S L H H P L E L I P A P E U N
E K M O E P E S C Y E R L F E Q M K D E
L P E J M S M H V C S C E I O A P M M E
M I I A Q A A O P R I S D N J T P P E L
E I X S T N E M E G A R U O C N E B N E
N E A K T K C H V H S K C O R R A E D U
Z O S R R L P C K E T V N T O Y T E F N
V V C K H P E W N L E K X R D E F D Q A
W O A E W P S S Y H S X O P R G U R Q M
E Y V S H B E P A A T R D N Q X L U Z M
M A H S I L E M U A S E A M J W O P A E
E T H I O P I A T H S L E N E M I E S L
```

1. This is the Lord's and all that is in it (Psalm 24:1)

E__ __ __ __

2. We should love them (Matthew 5:44)

E__ __ __ __ __ __

3. The kind of life Jesus offers (John 3:16)

E__ __ __ __ __ __

4. Book written by "the Teacher, the son of David, king in Jerusalem"

E__ __ __ __ __ __ __ __ __ __ __

5. This man, Methusaleh's dad, "walked with God; then he was no more, because God took him" (Genesis 5:24)

E__ __ __ __

6. Where God planted a garden (Genesis 2:8)
E_ _ _ _

7. Where Joseph was assistant ruler (Genesis 41:41)
E_ _ _ _ _

8. One of Joseph's sons; later a dominant tribe in Israel (Genesis 41:52)
E_ _ _ _ _ _

9. He called fire from heaven, then sat under a tree and moped (1 Kings 18–19)
E_ _ _ _ _

10. The New Testament has 21 of them E_ _ _ _ _ _ _

11. The Temanite who psychoanalyzed Job (Job 4)
E_ _ _ _ _ _

12. He bartered a birthright for a bowl of broth (Genesis 25:29–34) E_ _ _

13. He got a double share of Elijah's spirit (2 Kings 2:9)
E_ _ _ _ _

14. The Baptist's mom (Luke 1:13) E_ _ _ _ _ _ _

15. Mother of Seth and, well, everybody (Genesis 4:25)
E_ _

16. This name means "God with us" (Matthew 1:23)
E_ _ _ _ _ _ _

17. "Let no one despise your youth, but set the believers an _____ in speech and conduct, in love, in faith, in purity" (1 Timothy 4:12)
E_ _ _ _ _ _

18. Where two disciples were walking when the newly risen Jesus joined them (Luke 24:13–14) E_ _ _ _ _

19. Job title of Darius, Augustus, and Tiberius (Ezra 4:5, Luke 2:1, and Luke 3:1)
E_ _ _ _ _ _

20. Quality Barnabas was known for (Acts 4:36)
E_ _ _ _ _ _ _ _ _ _ _

21. Where Candace was queen (Acts 8:27) E_ _ _ _ _ _ _

It's All Relative

> *Draw a line from the people in the left column to a brother or sister in the right column. Then circle all 24 names in the puzzle. Answers on page 77.*

```
B D I V A D A N D R E W S
O N A R E B E N J A M I N
C I B M S J E O A N E V E
A A E A A O S I M O N E B
J C L R U E L I A B A L E
A O H T P A R O N L A E U
M D A H A Y R A M H R A R
E L M A I R I M C O O H H
S H E M R A C H E L N J M
```

Aaron	Abel
Cain	Absalom
David	Andrew
Jacob	Benjamin
James	Eliab
Joseph	Esau
Leah	Ham
Levi	John
Mary	Martha
Shem	Miriam
Simon	Rachel
Solomon	Rueben

Miracles didn't only happen in the New Testament. There were many miracles in the Old Testament too. Fill in the missing vowels (a, e, i, o, u), and then solve the puzzle by finding the 26 entries. Answers on page 77.

B__l__ __m   F__sh   L__ __ns   R__d S__ __

Bl__ __d   Fl__ __r   M__nn__   R__ck

C__rm__l   F__rn__c__   M__s__s   R__d

D__nk__y   J__n__h   N__m__ __n   S__n

__l__j__h   J__rd__n   __ __l   W__t__r

__l__sh__   J__sh__ __   Q__ __ __l

F__r__   L__pr__sy   R__v__ns

```
J  O  S  H  U  A  Y  E  K  N  O  D
R  A  V  E  N  S  L  J  O  N  A  H
E  W  A  T  E  R  O  H  G  E  B  J
D  M  W  C  A  R  M  E  L  L  Y  D
S  A  R  O  D  E  O  I  L  I  S  R
E  A  E  A  R  A  S  C  O  J  O  U
A  L  N  I  K  H  E  N  K  A  R  O
H  A  F  C  A  F  S  N  O  H  P  L
S  B  L  O  O  D  N  U  S  I  E  F
I  N  A  M  A  A  N  N  A  M  L  M
F  U  R  N  A  C  E  L  I  A  U  Q
```

A Time for Everything

B_ _ _   K_ _ _   R_ _ _ _ _ _

B_ _ _ _   K_ _ _   S_ _ _

B_ _ _ _   L_ _ _ _   S_ _

D_ _ _ _   L_ _ _   S_ _ _ _ _ _ _

D_ _   L_ _ _   S_ _ _ _ _

E_ _ _ _ _ _ M_ _ _ _   T_ _ _

G_ _ _ _ _   P_ _ _ _   T_ _ _ _

H_ _ _   P_ _ _ _   W_ _

H_ _ _   P_ _ _ _   W_ _ _

```
K  B  D  S  E  E  K  M  L  B  W  O  R  H  T  E  A  R
E  W  E  E  P  S  E  I  E  U  O  E  V  E  C  A  E  P
E  M  R  U  T  I  E  A  L  I  Q  M  G  P  I  F  S  B
P  E  B  E  D  L  K  W  P  L  L  O  L  J  R  J  P  O
E  S  R  R  T  E  C  N  A  D  R  U  G  A  T  H  E  R
T  O  E  N  A  N  F  E  T  A  C  R  I  Y  Z  E  A  N
A  L  A  N  S  C  A  D  W  K  T  N  A  L  P  A  K  X
H  C  K  H  O  E  E  H  G  U  A  L  E  V  O  L  W  A
```

After you have found the 28 words listed, decide on the puzzle's theme and write it below. Answers on page 78.

```
J  B  E  T  H  E  L  E  A  D  A  E  L  I  G  N
O  L  S  U  C  C  O  T  H  A  L  E  D  E  D  P
H  E  M  E  T  T  A  C  E  R  O  B  A  T  G  I
C  B  O  I  E  N  C  H  R  E  L  R  A  A  E  S
I  A  R  S  Z  D  H  R  M  E  G  I  D  D  O  G
R  N  I  E  D  I  O  I  O  L  H  E  R  E  B  A
E  O  A  V  E  M  R  S  N  Y  Q  U  S  I  E  H
J  N  H  I  R  L  J  E  C  A  R  M  E  L  N  O
E  F  O  L  A  E  S  O  G  T  N  U  T  N  O  R
S  N  E  O  Z  I  P  I  T  A  L  O  A  T  R  E
H  Y  A  R  N  M  B  A  R  R  G  A  I  L  B  B
C  U  E  A  D  E  A  V  Y  A  C  P  S  Z  E  O
O  E  I  T  O  U  C  P  D  R  A  S  R  E  H  Y
L  J  I  N  O  L  A  J  I  A  M  K  L  H  K  L
```

_ _ _ _ _ _ _ _ and _ _ _ _ _ _

Achor	Eshcol	Jericho	Pisgah
Aijalon	Gerizim	Jezreel	Salt
Ararat	Gibeon	Lebanon	Sinai
Baca	Gilead	Megiddo	Succoth
Bethel	Hebron	Moriah	Tabor
Carmel	Hermon	Nebo	Zared
Elah	Horeb	Olives	Zion

Gifts for Every Occasion

Many gifts were given in the Bible. Search for these 30 words, and then unscramble the leftover letters to reveal the mystery gift. Answers on page 78.

Almonds	Donkeys	Myrrh	Spices
Balm	Ewes	Offering	Spirit
Bowls	Goats	Oils	Time
Camels	Gold	Pans	Wares
Clothing	Honey	Perfume	Wealth
Copper	Horses	Rams	Weapons
Corban	Jewelry	Service	
Dishes	Mules	Silver	

```
B  A  L  M  S  W  E  A  L  T  H  E
K  L  A  U  N  A  B  R  O  C  M  J
W  M  S  L  P  R  D  H  L  U  R  E
E  O  I  E  A  O  F  O  F  A  C  W
A  N  L  S  N  E  T  R  M  N  A  E
P  D  V  K  S  H  E  S  T  R  C  L
O  S  E  C  I  P  S  E  E  I  I  R
N  Y  R  N  P  L  I  S  V  W  M  Y
S  N  G  O  I  H  R  R  Y  M  E  E
N  E  C  O  F  F  E  R  I  N  G  N
C  A  M  E  L  S  G  O  A  T  S  O
B  O  W  L  S  D  I  S  H  E  S  H
```

___ ___ ___ ___ ___ ___ ___ ___ ___ ___

In the Bible, people and things sometimes come in pairs. There are 32 words and names hidden in this puzzle, but we only give you 16 of them. You have to fill in the other part of each pair, and then find all 32 words in the puzzle. Answers on page 78.

```
Z  C  N  U  A  S  E  L  A  A  G  E  M  O  A  D
B  P  E  E  H  S  S  L  A  F  F  A  T  S  L  S
D  R  U  M  X  F  I  R  L  Y  T  Q  O  C  L  A
S  A  H  K  W  U  Z  K  P  L  E  K  H  D  I  C
E  U  P  T  Q  I  S  W  H  N  L  N  E  Z  C  K
H  M  A  A  E  F  D  A  E  X  L  O  Q  S  C
S  E  S  F  M  I  Y  F  G  P  I  J  L  H  I  L
A  L  J  A  I  W  L  S  E  L  A  E  V  D  R  O
O  I  J  O  Q  R  S  O  A  L  B  E  A  M  P  T
S  J  V  Q  S  T  E  H  G  A  I  V  V  G  J  H
A  A  Z  N  A  E  L  Y  T  H  I  S  A  E  A  P
L  H  N  O  R  W  P  L  R  D  J  D  H  S  C  A
I  C  G  Z  C  O  M  H  U  A  A  O  V  A  O  U
S  J  E  A  E  I  D  W  A  M  M  L  H  J  B  L
V  X  I  S  L  N  O  S  M  A  S  X  H  N  K  V
Y  N  G  K  O  B  R  I  M  S  T  O  N  E  L  B
```

Adam and
_ _ _

Alpha and
_ _ _ _ _

Aquila and
_ _ _ _ -
_ _ _ _ _

Cain and
_ _ _ _

_ _ _ _ _
and Goliath

_ _ _ _ -
_ _ _ and
Elisha

_ _ _ _
and Brim-
stone

Jacob and
_ _ _ _

James and
_ _ _ _

_ _ _ _ _
and Joseph

Milk and
_ _ _ _ _

_ _ _ _ _
and Silas

Rod and
_ _ _ _ _

Sackcloth and
_ _ _ _ _

_ _ _ _ -
_ _ _ and
Delilah

_ _ _ _ _
and Goats

Bible Word Search Puzzles ● 59

Dreams and Dreamers

Sometimes people in the Bible fell into a deep sleep and dreamed. After you have found all 35 dream-related words, the leftover letters will reveal the mystery word. Answers on page 79.

```
R  E  V  L  I  S  E  I  R  E  T  S  Y  M
S  H  E  E  T  S  I  M  A  G  E  S  A  O
I  E  N  Y  A  W  R  I  A  T  S  H  L  D
T  S  G  R  H  E  R  O  D  G  E  E  C  S
R  T  A  A  T  R  U  N  O  R  I  A  P  I
E  H  P  E  S  O  J  T  L  N  C  V  H  W
V  G  P  R  T  S  Y  R  A  M  O  E  C  E
E  U  T  H  S  A  E  D  B  T  W  S  E  T
L  O  S  T  A  N  I  M  A  L  S  I  L  L
A  H  U  P  E  R  E  Z  N  O  R  B  E  A
T  T  S  Y  B  W  A  R  N  I  N  G  M  D
I  L  E  G  N  A  B  O  C  A  J  O  I  D
O  N  J  E  P  R  O  P  H  E  S  Y  B  E
N  E  B  U  C  H  A  D  N  E  Z  Z  A  R
```

— — — — — — — — — — — —

Abimelech	Herod	Mary	Sheaves
Angel	Images	Messages	Sheets
Animals	Iron	Mysteries	Silver
Beasts	Jacob	Nebuchadnezzar	Stairway
Bronze	Jesus	Peter	Statue
Clay	Joseph	Pharaoh	Thoughts
Cows	Laban	Prophesy	Warning
Daniel	Ladder	Revelation	Wisdom
Egypt	Magi	Sarah	

Now match the dreamer with the dream:

1. Abimelech (Genesis 20:2–4)   a. stairway/ladder

2. Jacob (Genesis 28:12)   b. statue

3. Laban (Genesis 31:24)   c. cows

4. Joseph (Genesis 37:5–7)   d. Jacob

5. Daniel (Daniel 7:1–8)   e. Sarah

6. Peter (Acts 10:10–12)   f. sheaves

7. Pharaoh (Genesis 41:1–2)   g. Herod

8. Nebuchadnezzar (Daniel 2:31)   h. animals

9. Magi (Matthew 2:12)   i. beasts

Down by the C~~~~~~

All 24 words in this word search begin with the letter C. First take
the quiz to figure out what the words are. Answers on page 79.

1. The emperor's image was on this, which was shown to Jesus (Matthew 22:19–21) C__ __ __

2. Cornelius was one; another stood by the cross (Acts 10:1 and Matthew 27:54)
C__ __ __ __ __ __ __

3. The Persian ruler who let God's people go (2 Chronicles 36:23) C__ __ __ __

4. High priest who accused Jesus of blasphemy (Matthew 26:3–4) C__ __ __ __ __ __ __

5. Angelic beings whose images adorned the Tabernacle (Exodus 25:18) C__ __ __ __ __ __ __

6. Perhaps he tried to refrain from killing his brother, but he wasn't Abel (Genesis 4:8) C__ __ __

7. There are two of these books in the Old Testament C__ __ __ __ __ __ __ __

8. There are two epistles to these folks in the New Testament C__ __ __ __ __ __ __ __ __

9. One of two spies who recommended entering the Promised Land (Numbers 14:6–8) C__ __ __ __

10. According to 1 Timothy 3:15, "the household of God" C__ __ __ __ __

11. Aaron explained that the people gave him their gold jewelry, he threw it in the fire, and this thing came out (Exodus 32:4) C__ __ __

12. The garment that made Joseph's brothers see red (Genesis 37:3) C__ __ __

13. "Blessed are the peacemakers, for they will be called _____ of God" (Matthew 5:9) C__ __ __ __ __ __ __

14. Don't try to squeeze this through the eye of a needle, unless you're very rich (Matthew 19:24) C__ __ __ __

15. Moses came down the mountain with ten of them (Exodus 20)
C__ __ __ __ __ __ __ __ __ __

16. Where Jesus worked his first miracle and became the life of the party (John 2:1–12) C__ __ __

17. "If we _____ our sins, he who is faithful and just will forgive us our sins and cleanse us from all unrighteousness" (1 John 1:9) C__ __ __ __ __ __

18. Galilee city where Jesus did many miracles (Mark 1–4) C__ __ __ __ __ __ __

19. Mountain where Elijah won a sacrificing duel (1 Kings 18:20–46) C__ __ __ __ __

20. The centurion who wanted Peter to preach to him (Acts 10:21) C_ _ _ _ _ _ _ _

21. Jesus was one; so was Joseph (Mark 6:3; Matthew 13:55) C_ _ _ _ _ _ _ _

22. Capital punishment in Roman times (Matthew 10:38) C_ _ _ _

23. Wood used for much of the Temple, imported from Lebanon (1 Kings 6:14–18) C_ _ _ _

24. We should praise God with these instruments "clanging" and "clashing" (Psalm 150:5) C_ _ _ _ _ _

```
S L A B M Y C Y S T N E M D N A M M O C
C O R I N T H I A N S M U H A A Y I U S
H Y G G I X B W P S Y I U C C W C Z W S
U H I N A I L Q A M E T N A R A V S T I
R V A C T W A H Q C G O X A N X R L V A
C F A N K Z P K N Q I T D F E R C M I N
H L N O A A X R E R J E Y C B O E R E S
F P X C I C O R U J C H W Y M W T P G L
B C N A I C S T I O C G X R A C H A A U
Y Y C V A P N C K P O A A U C O A T S C
R U C W L E M R A Z A N M S K X V X S L
E I A C C T D I R L D R Y E J X R L E H
T C C T E N S S B M E S S O L A J B F Y
N H H Q E H C E E U N C I C N C S U N S
E I W W X A P L S J R B A I L X E Q O U
P L W N L A C C U O N E O Q S U H V C I
R D Z V R E F I O P R C H E S X X R K L
A R A F F T C N D C A C I C P L O F Q E
C E H G I C G O O K J F A B F S E P G N
Y N K U A H E R E I L Y V W S Y O U U R
Z X T I C A I H P C H U S S R X V Z A O
C Q N D T J X C U M F C A L E B S Q C C
```

A-OK

Take the quiz to figure out the 24 **A** entries in this word search.
Then find all those words. Answers on page 79.

```
R E G N A E H S A I H S S O I T N A Q A
B O M A A U G U S T U S X W A Q K C A X
I A S Z Y S W T B L S I E Q T S T Q R H
X U T G B K A Y S C W A Y G A D M W A E
U R S X A N E A L V G R D Q S O S O R A
Y C A N A Y S K S M E C U A E O W C A D
F M K N P S A C I T S R F O M F S V T Y
O Q I U Y D Z B L C G V T Q O Z T B Y Z
A A M R V E A G R E U S U J I W W K A R
S N A M P B Q B U A I L G C O D N N R W
F A A T K Y P U E R H Y A Y A D W E K G
I Y E N I J A K H D G A A D F H V G N M
D S A F A C P C A P N H M K A C A X Y Z
S L P A O V I U X N G E T P D A W B H X
U D C A I T S S I Y T K G S W U F A T S
T O U P N B H K N D A I E O W B B T S N
W P U A B A A A W J G H O Z J S O Z A E
G E A E A X N R S Y S H Z C A V X Q I H
A C R A Q N X B A A T U C L H M I C R T
T R C D A B T U F I H I L J Y S S Q Y A
A T M O N J J O B K U O A B Q Y G L S M
S L C O L A T R G N O X L K Q X W E S L
U E B Z R G E J Q C Y D A Y T D F K A R
H B J F Y E X L W U B M O L A S B A B W
M A N D J D N A M R E H S A G U I I S X
```

64 ☸ Bible Word Search Puzzles

1. He raised Cain (Genesis 4:1)
A__ __ __

2. First homicide victim (Genesis 4:8) A__ __ __

3. Where the ark parked (Genesis 8:4) A__ __ __ __ __

4. What a "harsh word stirs up" (Proverbs 15:1) A__ __ __ __

5. Where Paul went after his conversion (Galatians 1:17)
A__ __ __ __ __

6. One of three—no, four!—in the fiery furnace (Daniel 3:19)
A__ __ __ __ __ __ __

7. David's long-haired, rebellious son (2 Samuel 13–14)
A__ __ __ __ __ __

8. "The one who denies the Father and the Son" (1 John 2:22)
A__ __ __ __ __ __ __ __

9. Nation that made the ten tribes of Israel get lost (2 Kings 17:6) A__ __ __ __ __ __

10. David tried some, but it just weighed him down (1 Samuel 17:38) A__ __ __ __

11. Where the Jesus people were first called Christians (Acts 11:26) A__ __ __ __ __ __

12. Noah's navy (Genesis 6:14)
A__ __

13. The exciting sequel to Luke's Gospel A__ __ __

14. God said he would be "the ancestor of a multitude of nations" (Genesis 17:5)
A__ __ __ __ __ __

15. Elijah's enemy (1 Kings 18)
A__ __ __

16. His decree sent one famous couple to the city of David (Luke 2:1) A__ __ __ __ __ __ __

17. Sapphira's real estate partner (Acts 5) A__ __ __ __ __ __

18. Where Job sat (Job 2:8)
A__ __ __ __

19. He told Peter about Jesus (John 1:40–41) A__ __ __ __ __

20. "_____, and it will be given you" (Matthew 7:7)
A__ __

21. Where Paul found a shrine "To an unknown god" (Acts 17:23) A__ __ __ __ __

22. Elisha made one float (2 Kings 6:5–6) A__ __ __ __ __

23. She blessed a special baby (Luke 2:36) A__ __ __

24. This son of Jacob had a name that means "Happy" (Genesis 30:13) A__ __ __ __

Old Books

Crammed into this square are the names of all the books of the Old Testament. See how many you can find. If you need help, consult the table of contents in your Bible. (Note: Samuel, Kings, and Chronicles are listed once each so there are 36 entries in this puzzle.) Answers on page 80.

```
H K N A H U M E K H A I M E H E N X W J
A S R E B M U N P R S I S E N E G N M O
G X S P R K A I E G J E T V D O O D M B
G M D K V M I H S E R W T F H M X G I E
A J L D O Z T N R A I I D K O Z U R C C
I M B S E S K E G Q I X Q L Z H S F A C
S A V A E U M L L S J A O T E O N G H L
U L B A Z I T E J P G S H J C S O D D E
C A F D A E I E J O F N O T H E I G Z S
I C J H T K P O R O S O W C A A T S Y I
T H H U E T N H G O I H O I R H A G D A
I I U Z D A Y N A P N B U C I Z T X A S
V H E X H G O L H N K O I A A A N N N T
E A K W S S E A O F I X M H H J E P I E
L I Z A R M B S E E S A T Y X O M P E S
D D F Z R A W X Z A A U H T D E A W L O
U A P B K Z O R M N R B U G A L L K K Q
F B Z K R D E U P R O V E R B S H E M D
A O U W U E E B Q Z Z S M L A S P I C D
G K S S O L D M S E L C I N O R H C M V
```

On the Job (from page 4)

Sea You Later (from page 5)

There's Music in the Air (from page 6)

Gift Rap (from page 7)

It's Empty (from page 6)

Tree's Company (from page 8)

Animal Planet (from page 9)

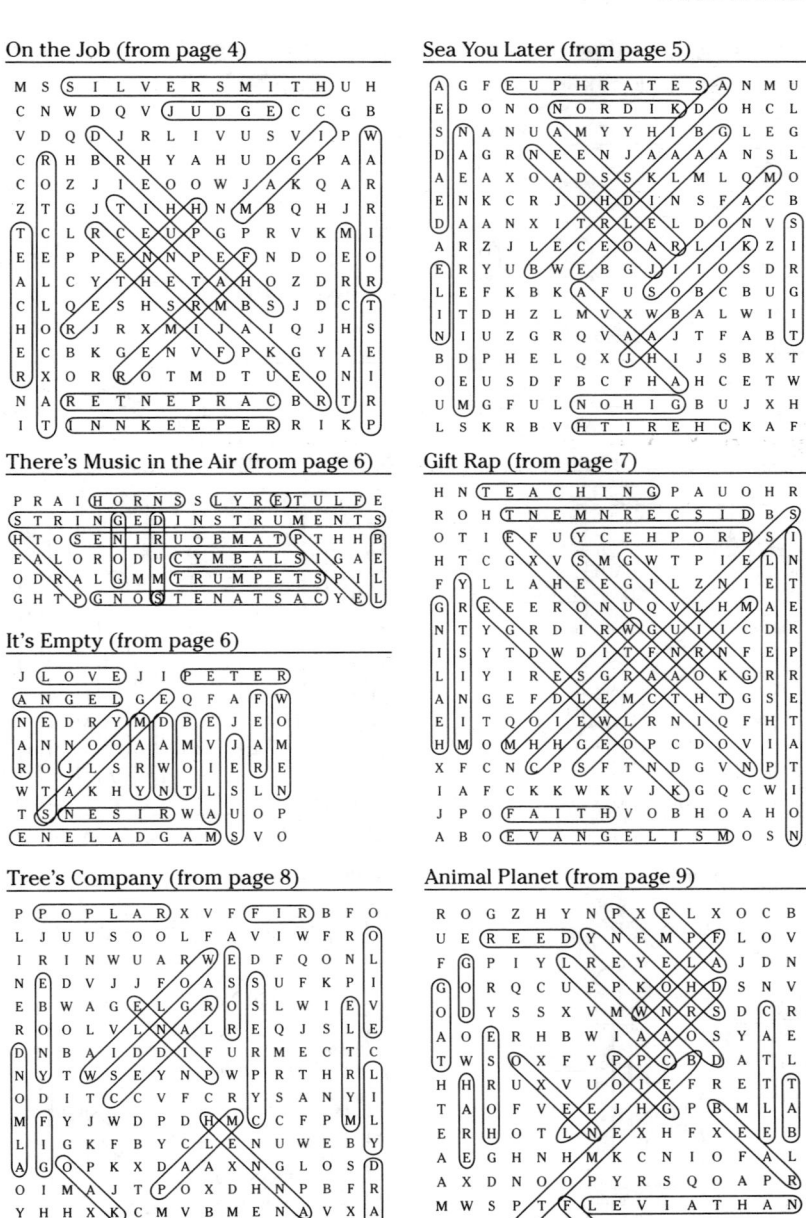

Answers

The Traveling Man (from page 10)

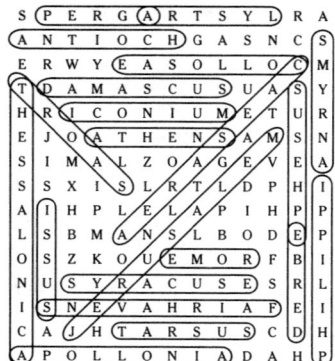

I Am . . . (from page 11)

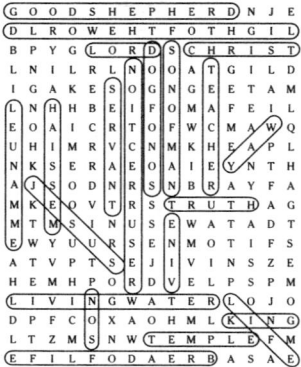

Tremendous *T*'s (from page 12)

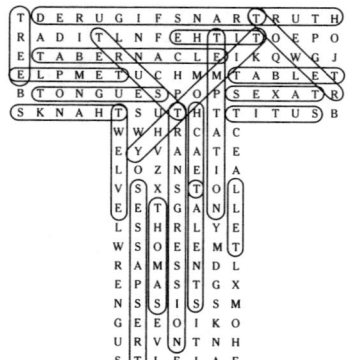

Powerful *P*'s (from page 13)

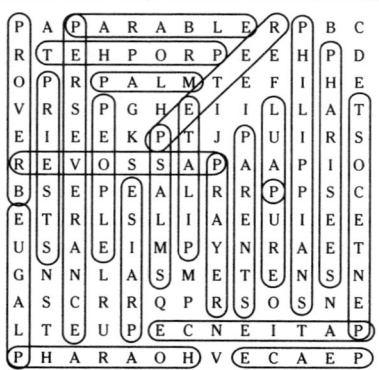

Follow Me (from page 14)

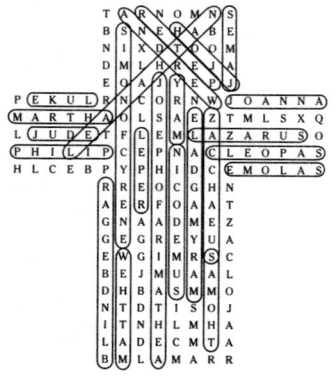

In the House (from page 15)

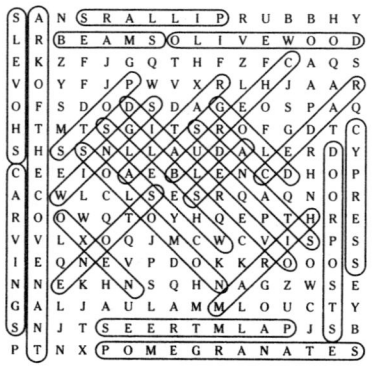

Good Old Moses (from page 16)

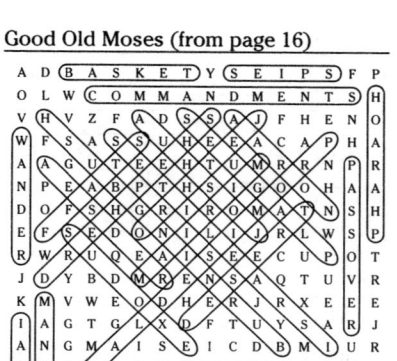

Fire, Writing, and Lions (from page 17)

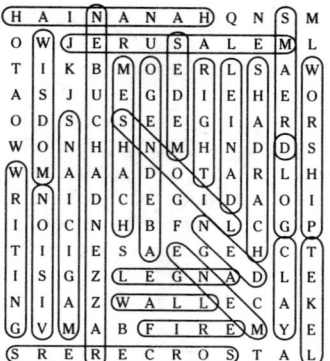

Earth, Wind, and Fire (from page 18)

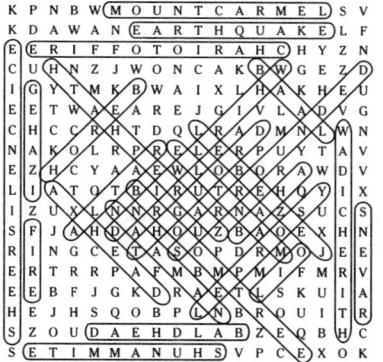

Ruth or Dare (from page 19)

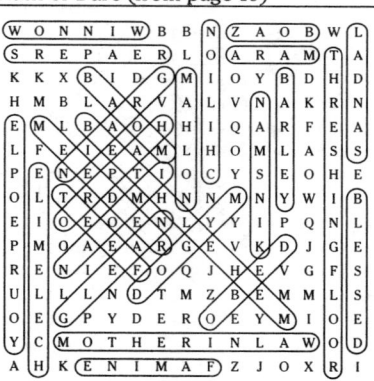

Jumping Jehoshaphat! (from page 20)

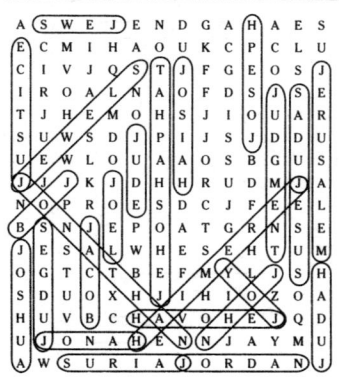

The Experience Was in Tents (from page 21)

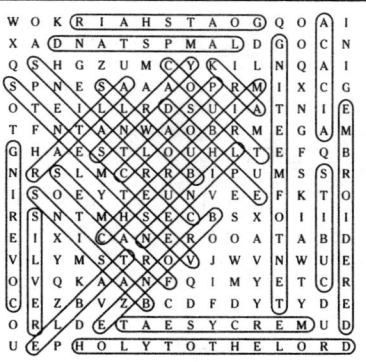

Answers

Singer Slinger (from page 22)

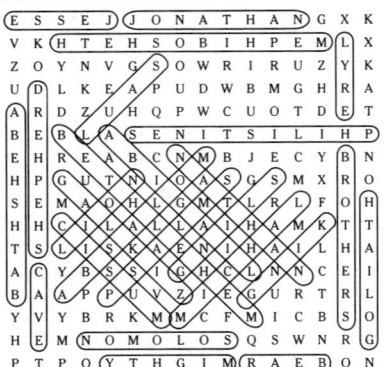

Crown Me! (from page 23)

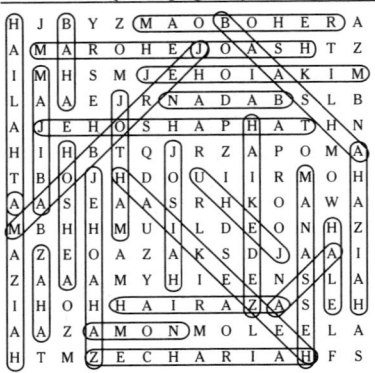

Not Your Average Joe (from page 24)

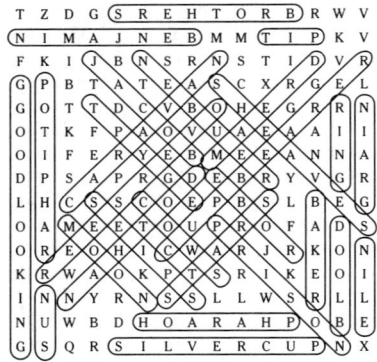

Family Tree (from page 25)

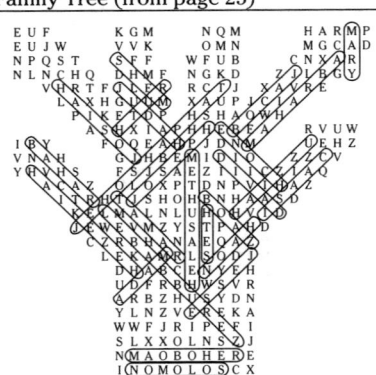

Earthly Stories with Heavenly Meanings (from page 26)

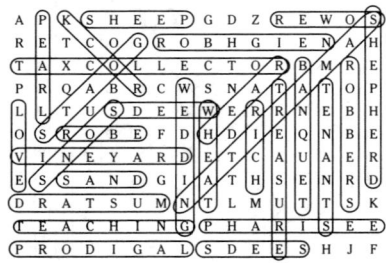

O Come, All Ye Faithful (from page 27)

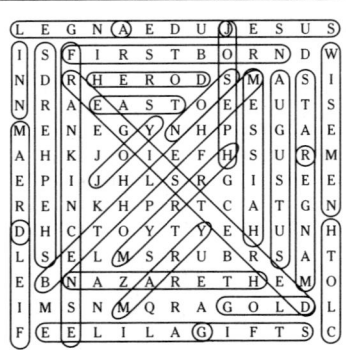

Super S's (from page 28)

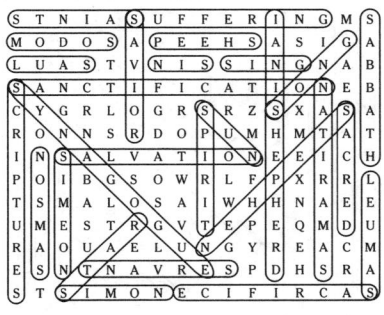

The Floating Zoo (from page 29)

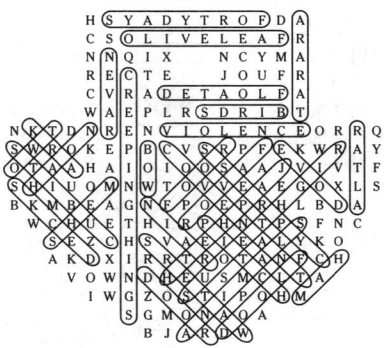

The Gospel Truth (from page 30)

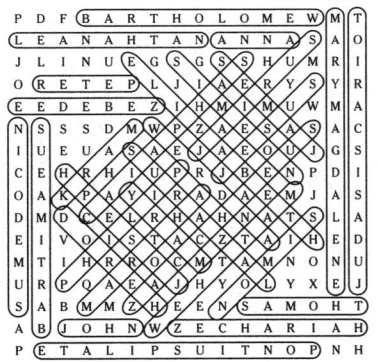

Church Chat (from page 31)

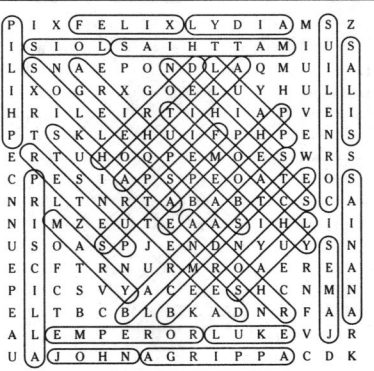

Eat, Drink, and Be Satisfied (from page 32)

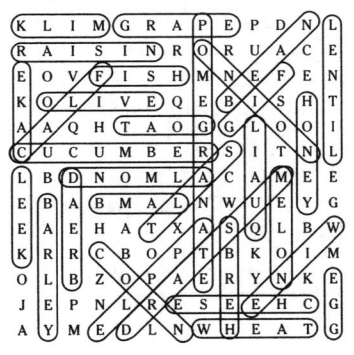

Chief of Staff (from page 33)

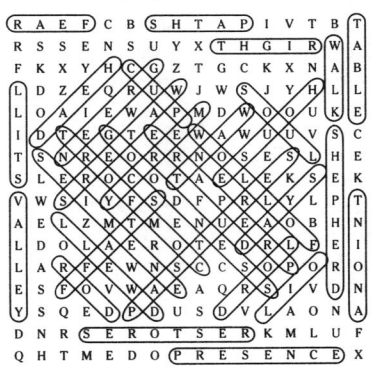

Answers

Awesome Happenings (from page 34)

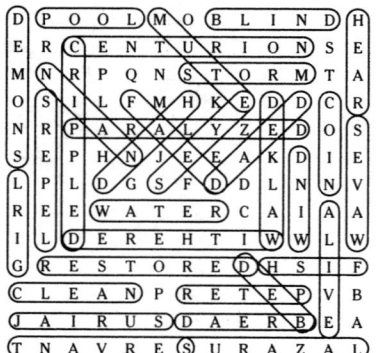

My Three Dads (from page 35)

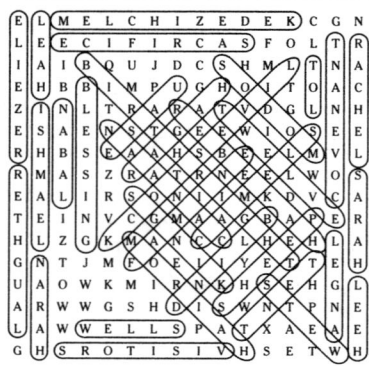

First Folks (from page 36)

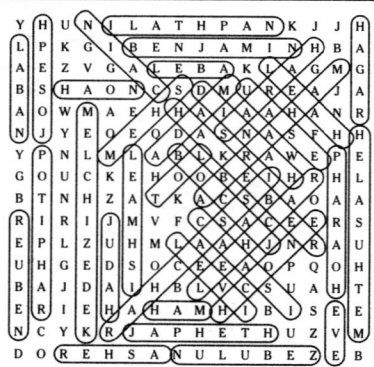

A Land of Many Tribes (from page 37)

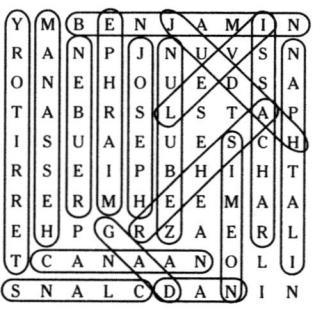

Palestine

Getting from Here to There (from page 38)

Camel
Cart
Chariot
Colt
Donkey
Horse
Mule
Oxen
Raft
Row Boats
Running
Sail Boats

Ships
Wagon
Walking

May You Always Be Blessed (from page 39)

Blessed
Glad
God
Heaven
Hunger
Inherit
Kingdom
Merciful
Poor
Prophets
Pure
Rejoice

Spirit
Thirst

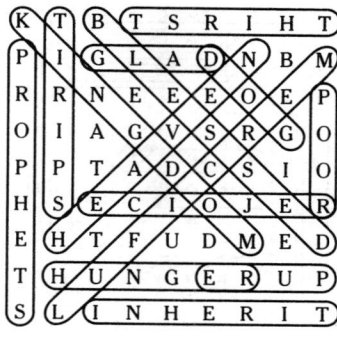

Top Ten List (from page 40)

You shall have no other gods before me.

You shall not make for yourself an idol.

You shall not make wrongful use of the name of the Lord.

Remember the sabbath day, and keep it holy.

Honor your father and your mother.

You shall not murder.

You shall not commit adultery.

You shall not steal.

You shall not bear false witness against your neighbor.

You shall not covet your neighbor's house... or anything that belongs to your neighbor.

Jesus Was Here (from page 41)

Bethany
Bethlehem
Bethphage
Bethsaida
Caesarea
Cana
Capernaum
Emmaus
Jericho
Jerusalem
Korazin
Magdala

Nain
Nazareth
Sychar
Tyre

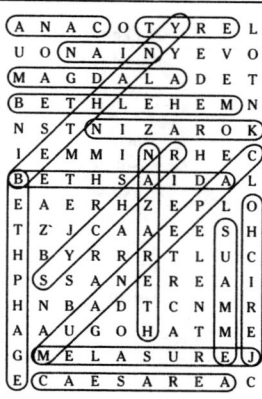

Answers

God's Daughters (from page 42)

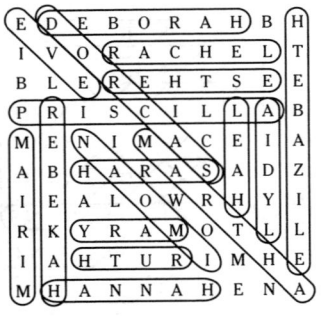

Biblical Women

Like Father, Like Son (from page 43)

Patriarch

New Books (from page 44)

Acts	Peter
Colossians	Philemon
Corinthians	Philippians
Ephesians	Revelation
Galatians	Romans
Hebrews	Thessalonians
James	Timothy
John	Titus
Jude	
Luke	
Mark	
Matthew	

Jonah Makes a U-Turn (from page 45)

Angry	Sackcloth
Ashes	Sacrifice
Belly	Sea
Bush	Ship
Deliverance	Storm
Evil	Swallow
Fish	Tarshish
Jonah	Thanksgiving
Joppa	Three
King	Wind
Love	Worm
Ninevah	

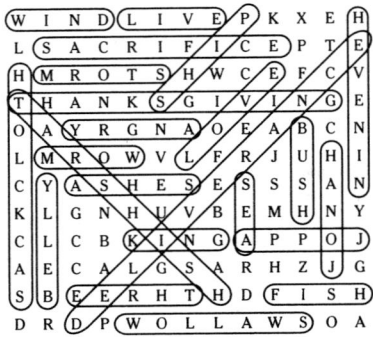

Fairest in the Land (from page 46)

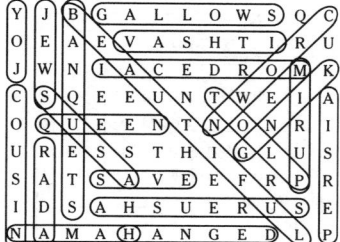

Queen Esther

Fun and Prophets (from page 47)

Agabus	John
Amos	Jonah
Daniel	Malachi
Elijah	Micah
Elisha	Nahum
Ezekiel	Nathan
Habakkuk	Obadiah
Haggai	Zechariah
Hosea	Zephaniah
Isaiah	
Jeremiah	
Joel	

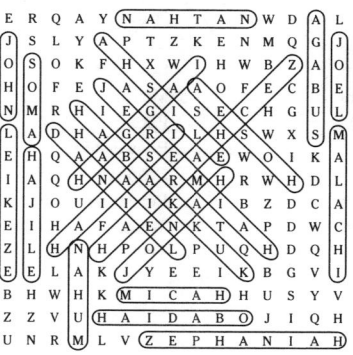

Busy B (from pages 48–49)

1. Bethlehem	14. Baker
2. Boat	15. Blood
3. Belshazzar	16. Babylon
4. Boaz	17. Baal
5. Begging	18. Baptizing
6. Blind	19. Babel
7. Bread	20. Bear
8. Barnabas	
9. Breath	
10. Benjamin	
11. Barabbas	
12. Branches	
13. Beroea	

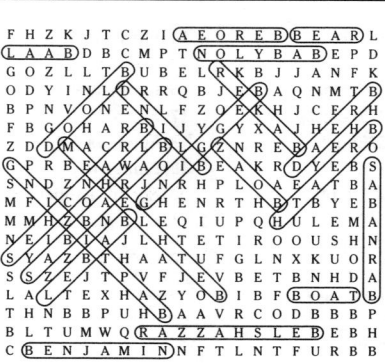

Answers

What's in a Name? (from page 50)

Abram	Abraham
Daniel	Belteshazzar
Hadassah	Esther
Hananiah	Shadrach
Jacob	Israel
Levi	Matthew
Mishael	Meshach
Nathanael	Bartholomew
Sarai	Sarah
Saul	Paul
Simon	Peter

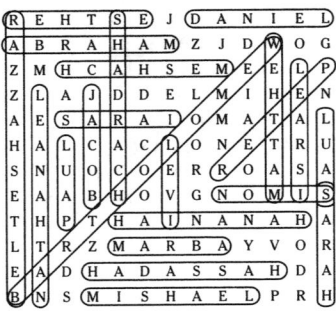

The Greatest Is . . . (from page 51)

Abide	Irritable
Angels	Kind
Bears	Love
Believe	Mirror
Boast	Patient
Ends	Possessions
Endures	Prophecies
Face	Rejoices
Faith	Tongues
Fully	Truth
Greatest	
Hope	

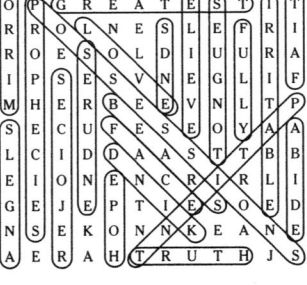

The E's Have It (from pages 52–53)

1. Earth	14. Elizabeth
2. Enemies	15. Eve
3. Eternal	16. Emmanuel
4. Ecclesiastes	17. Example
5. Enoch	18. Emmaus
6. Eden	19. Emperor
7. Egypt	20. Encouragement
8. Ephraim	21. Ethiopia
9. Elijah	
10. Epistles	
11. Eliphaz	
12. Esau	
13. Elisha	

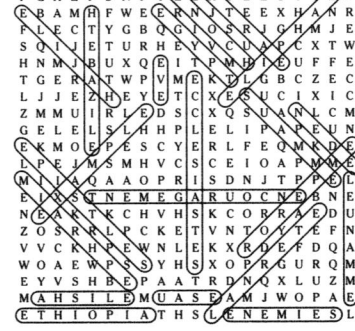

It's All Relative (from page 54)

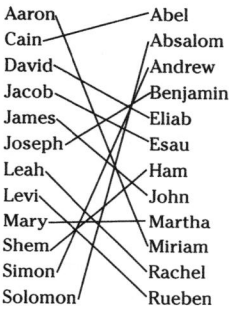

Aaron, Cain, David, Jacob, James, Joseph, Leah, Levi, Mary, Shem, Simon, Solomon

Abel, Absalom, Andrew, Benjamin, Eliab, Esau, Ham, John, Martha, Miriam, Rachel, Rueben

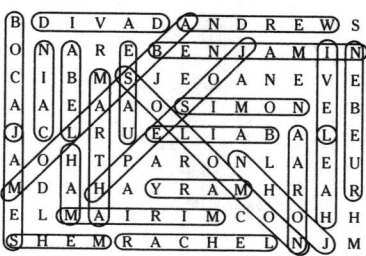

It's Unbelievable! (from page 55)

Balaam
Blood
Carmel
Donkey
Elijah
Elisha
Fire
Fish
Flour
Furnace
Jonah
Jordan
Joshua
Leprosy
Lions
Manna
Moses
Namaan
Oil
Quail
Ravens
Red Sea
Rock
Rod
Sun
Water

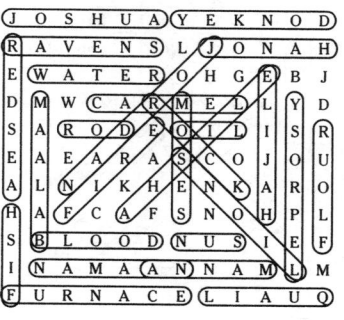

A Time for Everything (from page 56)

Born
Break
Build
Dance
Die
Embrace
Gather
Hate
Heal
Keep
Kill
Laugh
Lose
Love
Mourn
Peace
Plant
Pluck
Refrain
Seek
Sew
Silence
Speak
Tear
Throw
War
Weep

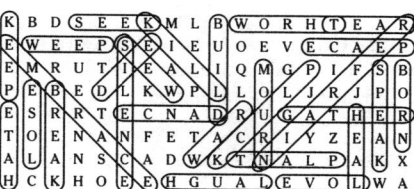

Answers

Ups and Downs (from page 57)

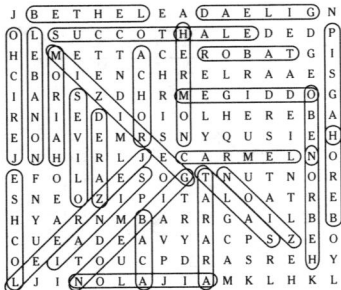

Mountains and Valleys

Gifts for Every Occasion (from page 58)

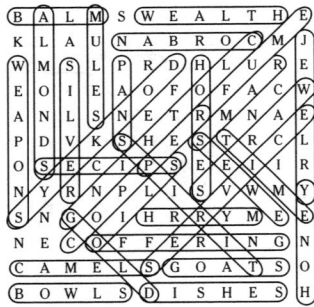

Frankincense

Me Two! (from page 59)

Adam and Eve
Alpha and Omega
Aquila and Priscilla
Cain and Abel
David and Goliath
Elijah and Elisha
Fire and Brimstone
Jacob and Esau
James and John
Mary and Joseph
Milk and Honey
Paul and Silas

Rod and Staff
Sackcloth and Ashes
Samson and Delilah
Sheep and Goats

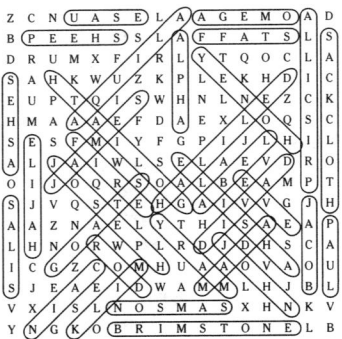

Dreams and Dreamers (from pages 60–61)

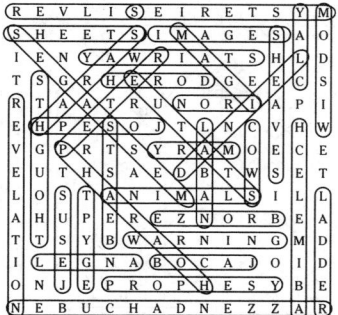

1 e; 2 a; 3 d; 4 f; 5 i; 6 h; 7 c; 8 b; 9 g

Interpretation

Down by the C (from pages 62–63)

1. Coin	14. Camel
2. Centurion	15. Commandments
3. Cyrus	16. Cana
4. Caiaphas	17. Confess
5. Cherubim	18. Capernaum
6. Cain	19. Carmel
7. Chronicles	20. Cornelius
8. Corinthians	21. Carpenter
9. Caleb	22. Cross
10. Church	23. Cedar
11. Calf	24. Cymbals
12. Coat	
13. Children	

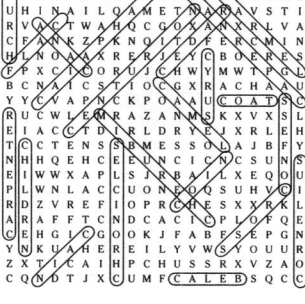

A-OK (from pages 64–65)

1. Adam	14. Abraham
2. Abel	15. Ahab
3. Ararat	16. Augustus
4. Anger	17. Ananias
5. Arabia	18. Ashes
6. Abednego	19. Andrew
7. Absalom	20. Ask
8. Antichrist	21. Athens
9. Assyria	22. Ax Head
10. Armor	23. Anna
11. Antioch	24. Asher
12. Ark	
13. Acts	

Bible Word Search Puzzles ● 79

Answers

Old Books (from page 66)

Amos
Chronicles
Daniel
Deuteronomy
Ecclesiastes
Esther
Exodus
Ezekiel
Ezra
Genesis
Habakkuk
Haggei
Hosea
Isaiah

Jeremiah
Job
Joel
Jonah
Joshua
Judges
Kings
Lamentations
Leviticus
Malachi
Micah
Nahum
Nehemiah
Numbers

Obadiah
Proverbs
Psalms
Ruth
Samuel
Song of Solomon
Zechariah
Zephaniah

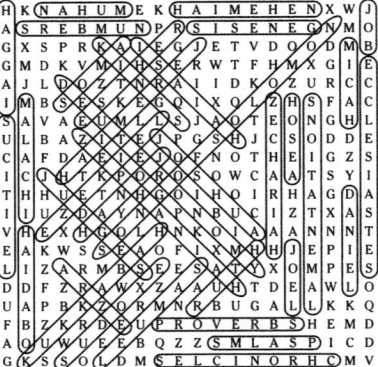